An excellent methodology overview ar
experienced executive coach. A stimul
approaches, developed and mastered
Andrew Green, Partner, Gallup

A great practical coaching book for coaches that offers a variety of
new insights, tools, models and that coaches can use and practise on
growing their coaching career and enable them to bring more value to
their clients.
**Nehad Tadros, Professional Certified Coach; President ICF United
Arab Emirates Chapter**

As a leader without any coaching qualifications, I found this
book incredibly helpful in providing a range of practical tools and
techniques that I could deploy with my team where personal growth
and change is the imperative. From working with the conscious mind
to getting deep into the soul, this book will definitely help me better
deploy strategies that best fit the person and challenge at hand.
**Tracy Clarke, CEO Europe and Americas and CEO Private Banking,
Standard Chartered Bank**

A truly thought-provoking and illuminating guide. Offering the reader
powerful frameworks, models and ways of approaching our coaching
client's needs. I love the way the content flows and connects together
with the underlying theme of exploring our five levels – from the
conscious mind through to the soul. The case studies resonated
with me, as if I were an observer of a deep and meaningful coaching
session. I am still reflecting upon 'George' from the book's final
chapter. My key take-away is to be reminded of how very deep and
extremely transformative coaching can be.
**Nigel Cumberland, The Silk Road Partnership – is an international
executive coach, mentor, facilitator and author of a range of leadership
and self-help books**

Elegantly written, simple to follow and apply, its intellectual applicability
is perhaps its strongest point: steps, guides, scenarios and ways of
using the techniques, *makes this the coach's swiss-army knife.*
**Perry Timms, Founder and CEO (Chief Energy Officer) of People &
Transformational HR (PTHR) – *HR Magazine's* Fifth Most Influential
Thinker 2018, TEDx speaker, author and international consultant**

As a systemic team coach well versed in integral leadership, I found
this book very useful in terms of the rich tools available that one can
use in their coaching practice with clients. I particularly enjoyed the

focus on the inner self and the attached experiential exercises with powerful tips and real-world practice with clients.
Bernard Chanliau, Professional Certified Coach, ICF; ICF Ireland Coach of the Year 2015

The coaching industry has generated a vast range of reference books for aspiring and newly-qualified coaches, as well as those coaches with intermediary experience. There aren't many written specifically for senior practitioners and this book is a welcome contribution to this genre. Each chapter offers a different approach, inviting coaches to go deeper with their clients to achieve transformative and lasting positive impact as well as continuing to reflect on their own practice. A thought-provoking book. I encourage all senior experienced coaches to read it.
Annabel Harper MA, FRSA, Change Connections Ltd

This book is both transforming and liberating. I can testify to the fact that the interventions contained in it enable deep and sustainable change. These were both key factors in my personal transformation to a different and more productive way of being.
Paul Morrish, Group Director Succession Wealth

Making a quantum leap in leadership performance is now achievable through this complete approach to changing and developing leadership impact. In particular, I found listening through the emotions and perspectives of others struck a chord with my own development as a leader and was critical to understanding how to communicate the way I made decisions.
Mike Rees, Founder at Strategic Vitality

There are many books on coaching; however, this one stands out. It is a treasure trove of practical and powerful techniques for advanced coaches that you can use to transform your clients, generating deep self-awareness, insights and personal growth, as well as improved performance and results. I would highly recommend this book to all those with a deep interest and curiosity in taking their coaching practice to the next level and enjoying self-discovery in the process.
James Brook, Leadership Psychologist, Executive Coach and Founder of Tech Talent Solutions Ltd

An immensely practical insight into first-class coaching skills. A must-read for all professional coaches looking to perfect their technique.
Nigel Jeremy, Chief Learning Officer, British Airways

THE JOURNEY INSIDE

THE JOURNEY INSIDE

INSIDE

Coaching to the Core

Edited by
Veronica Munro

Contributing Authors
Veronica Munro, Richard Haggerty,
Shirley Attenborough, Dan Newby,
David Ross, Colin D. Smith and Aidan Tod

Practical Inspiration
PUBLISHING

First published in Great Britain by Practical Inspiration Publishing, 2019

© Veronica Munro, 2019

The moral rights of the author have been asserted

ISBN   978-1-78860-114-6 (print)
       978-1-78860-113-9 (epub)
       978-1-78860-112-2 (mobi)

Front and back cover photograph by Leo Roomets

Every effort has been made to trace copyright holders and to obtain their permission for the use of copyright material. The publisher apologizes for any errors or omissions and would be grateful if notified of any corrections that should be incorporated in future reprints or editions of this book.

EDITOR'S NOTE

Early in 2018 I invited six independent world-class executive coaches to partner with me, and each other, and create this book. I had known them all separately for several years. They had each created their own unique coaching interventions, models, practices and sets of skills and I had the privilege to study and work with them (and others) during my journey as a professional coach. With their contributions and inputs to my learnings I was able to transform myself, my coaching practice and also the lives of many of my clients and those they touched too (both professionally and personally).[1]

My goal with this book is to share some of our collective work with you and other coaches and leaders around the world who wish to continue to learn, develop and grow themselves and, by doing so, keep at the top of their game and stay relevant as the world continues to evolve and change.

What came as a great surprise to me, and what I was not expecting in our journey together, was the huge amount of collaboration that grew between all the authors as they read and re-read each other's chapters, offering suggested edits, rewrites, word changes and structural improvements.

It has been a fun and highly productive journey, and a huge privilege, working with Shirley, Colin, Dan, David and Aidan and of course Richard who has been our linchpin and go-to guy at all times. We wouldn't have made it this far without him! Thank you all!

---

[1] All examples in this book are based on real-life cases but with names and details changed to maintain anonymity.

Thank you too to our publisher Alison Jones for all her inspired insights in bringing this book to life.

Veronica Munro

EVERY CONTACT LEAVES A TRACE[1]

CONTENTS

FIGURES

TABLES

INTRODUCTION

Leaders and organisations at the top of their game are always seeking coaches who work at the top of theirs. They are looking for experts who can take them to places they have never been, discovered or uncovered before; places that enable them to transform who they are and the people and organisations around them.

This book takes you on a series of inspiring journeys deep within yourself, and if you are up to the challenge, with your coaching clients too. Each expert contributor shares new insights, tools, models and practices that are *proven accelerators* which transform the results a coach can achieve at the highest levels within organisations and within society – results that are sustainable and put you, and your clients, at the top of their game.

This is a pragmatic, practical book for all coaches and leaders who have an interest in how to facilitate change in their organisations: a book that provides some of the most advanced and unique coaching techniques from a select group of international executive coaches who support leaders to transform their businesses and their lives.

The transformational techniques shared here are ready to use for practising coaches, wherever you are on your journey. They are also great resources for anyone who wants to coach, lead and mentor, as part of their role within an organisation. Throughout the book we use the word 'client' as a way to refer to anyone you are coaching: an external client, colleague or member of staff.

Our aim as coaches is always to generate sustainable change for our clients, to enable new patterns of behaviour and thinking to become automatic, becoming a natural and integrated part of daily life. This kind of change can only happen when we go below the surface, to the deeper levels of their psyche, where the client can explore and rework their inner terrain.

You'll discover in this book uniquely designed techniques at five different and deepening levels within the human psyche, to enable you to help your clients achieve this substantive and sustainable level of change.

The five levels we are working with in this book are:

1. The Conscious Mind
2. The Unconscious Mind
3. The Emotions
4. The Identity
5. The Soul.

INVITATION

We invite you to journey with us as we travel into, and through, the depths of those psyches we work with, and demonstrate how you can use these techniques with your clients and make a real and lasting difference to their lives.

Welcome along!

Veronica Munro

I

THE CONSCIOUS MIND

Covered in this section

We always meet a client where they are in their thinking by pacing their conscious understanding of the challenges they face and the outcomes they wish to achieve.

By conscious, we mean that part of the mind used for logic, processing, reasoning, structuring ideas, rationalisation and analysis. When we initially engage with clients, we are engaging at this conscious level. It is a starting point for all our interactions, though not the end point. Clients come to us with a problem, challenge, issue or outcome that they can consciously articulate, though they typically do not have an understanding of the unconscious drivers of these, or indeed how to resolve them.

Change typically begins with consciously thinking about new behaviours and regular practice of these resulting from the coaching.

In this section, there are three chapters that introduce you to a variety of ways to work powerfully with clients at this level and deepen their understanding and awareness of their challenges and the impact of these, so that they can create new plans of action to resolve them. As coaches, it is also true that whilst working at this conscious level, the deepening awareness and shifts in our clients start to occur at the unconscious level as well.

Chapter 1: Turn Your Challenge Inside OUT: The Physical Metaphor Technique
Veronica Munro and Richard Haggerty

This creative technique is used to enable clients to get outside of their heads, and their current thinking, where they often find themselves stuck. The technique, developed from the ancient practices of military war games, enables clients to externalise their challenges and outcomes, and experiment creatively using everyday objects to more freely discover different strategies, options and solutions.

Chapter 2: Take the Plunge and Dive Deeper using Transactional Analysis
Shirley Attenborough

Shirley takes us through the practical use of Transactional Analysis and related tools to encourage clients to consciously explore the deeper levels inside themselves and make more effective shifts in their behaviours to achieve the results they desire.

Chapter 3: The Transformational Impact of Active Listening
Colin D. Smith

Colin shares with us guiding principles in building the skills and awareness of Active Listening and where to focus our attention, so that we can build the level of relationships with clients that can lead to change beyond conscious levels of being.

CHAPTER 1

TURN YOUR CHALLENGE INSIDE OUT

The Physical Metaphor Technique

Veronica Munro and Richard Haggerty

A powerful and systematic hands-on technique for clients to take a challenge, externalise it, and develop new perspectives and strategies that allow them to notice opportunities so they can take concrete steps to move forward. This enables their conscious minds to access creative ideas that are outside their current awareness.

Covered in this chapter

- An engaging 'hands-on' process that is client-led
- How to use the physical environment to represent challenges and identify new strategies and actions
- The power of pre-framing to create full engagement from clients
- Dissociating from a challenge to get new viewpoints and solutions
- How to create a completely safe space for clients where there is no fear of failure

---

INTRODUCTION

Military war games started as games not dissimilar to chess in fifth-century Ancient Greece, and then later in Northern India. These evolved into battlefield simulations during the seventeenth and eighteenth centuries, and later into highly sophisticated military and economic war games across a range of organisations, industries and countries.

Conducting war games in the Napoleonic era, for instance, was a way of determining the best means to prevail given the known circumstances about an enemy location, and then look at possible options and strategies for fighting a battle. It introduced realism into the decision-making process so that when it was time to engage, the strategy which had the greatest chances of success had already been theoretically tried and tested, and could be implemented with confidence. The Physical Metaphor Technique (PMT) is a development of this tool in the context of coaching.

The purpose of the PMT is to facilitate a client to move from a challenge they have, through the use of this visual hands-on approach, to creating different scenarios and strategies, until they reach their outcome.

The PMT is designed to help your client identify new ideas, approaches, strategies and options to seemingly entrenched challenges. This can be achieved by using any immediate space in the environment around a client as a metaphor, and landscape, for the challenges, resources and potential solutions. In this way, it acts as a natural bridge to the client's creative unconscious resources and solutions, and bypasses the sometimes more rigid limited thinking of the conscious mind. It is a powerful technique that assists the analytical part of the mind to work with much more freedom, whilst at the same time creating opportunities for clients to gain creative insights spontaneously from deeper levels of consciousness. This begins the journey within.

BENEFITS OF THE PHYSICAL METAPHOR TECHNIQUE IN COACHING

The PMT provides a safe space for clients to externalise the challenge, or situation, as a physically represented metaphor. This naturally dissociates the client from the challenge and any emotions attached, so they can witness what is happening more clearly. From this 'third position,' or alternative perspective, the client is able to look at the situation, unencumbered by past judgements and emotions. This allows fresh perspectives to come to mind and is more conducive to developing and testing a range of strategies and solutions with a sense of freedom.

Some of the challenges, and more complex areas, this particular intervention can help clients with are:

- Creating new winning strategies to beat the competition
- Identifying new streams of business or products within a highly competitive market
- Scoping out the opportunities and gaps in the market from different perspectives
- Building a successful strategy for the acquisition of another business / company
- Identifying different approaches for shifting the culture / organisational structure to achieve a significant edge over the competition
- Reviewing 360-degree feedback received from selected stakeholders across the organisation and working on the new behaviours required to meet their success criteria in selected areas.

PRE-FRAMING AND THE 7 STEP PROCESS

Pre-framing

'Framing' here refers to creating the context, and setting a strong intention: a lens or lenses through which the activities can be experienced. Establishing frames ahead of a coaching session (pre-framing) enables the coach to avoid common misunderstandings so the client interprets what is happening in a specific way, or set of ways. Setting clear frames (of reference) upfront can also make a new activity more clear, purposeful and enjoyable. It is, therefore, a powerful way to help the client to become more motivated and focused on the task in hand.

Pre-frames serve important functions. They:

- Establish rapport
- Create a sense of safety
- Establish credibility for the exercise
- Amplify motivation
- Create agreement to participate.

Gaining agreement from the client, before you start this technique, is essential. This primes your client to be thinking, 'This could really help me and is worthy of my time and energy.' They will also want to know that this is a technique they can experiment with in any way they wish, with any challenge they have. There are no right or wrong moves, only different strategies and options.

As you begin, offer some frames of reference upfront (pre-frames) that you feel match your client's needs, and gain agreement. (Note: examples of words spoken by the coach are in italics for ease of reference.)

Examples of effective pre-frames and follow-up questions include:

Exploration frame

- *Today, we are going to focus on you exploring and generating a range of strategies and solutions to your challenge. There will be a variety of these, and there are no right or wrong ones. Your role is to explore these and identify the most appropriate ones to achieve your outcome. OK?*

Control frame

- *Some people get stuck and don't realise when their thinking is 'inside the box.' Today we are literally going to go 'outside the box.' You will be in control every step of the way, and I will just be checking in to make sure you are happy with each step of the process. How does that sound?*

Scientist frame

- *This process stops the cycle of stressful thinking by moving everything to the 'outside.' It stops the challenge in the way it currently is, and allows you scope to experiment with new ways of moving forward. How does having new ways to approach things sound?*

Risk-free frame

- *If you could explore this challenge in a totally different way that made it easier to identify challenge points and test out new strategies and solutions with zero risks, would that be something you are interested in exploring?*

Flexibility frame

- *Everything that you try can be changed at any time. You are in total control and all your ideas can be modified or ruled out as you wish. Like a child playing with Lego, you get to create, build and change things in any way you want.*

Confidentiality frame

- *To support what we are doing, I will take photos of the scenes as they develop and include these in your confidential Coaching Report following this session. This means that you don't have to think about remembering each step or insight. Is this OK with you?*

A more in-depth explanation of reframing and its role in coaching can be found in Chapter 4: 'Breaking Free: Unlocking Doors with Deep Reframing' by Richard Haggerty.

THE 7 STEP PHYSICAL METAPHOR TECHNIQUE

Step 1: Elicit challenge and outcomes

With frames properly established, you can now take time to identify the challenge and outcomes.

You are specifically looking for:

- The challenge they have now
- Why it is a problem for them (the stress, emotion, difficulty etc.)
- The impact and consequences of this challenge on the client, on other people and within the organisation.

At this point, we want the client to connect to their challenge in a way that motivates them to want to move away from the potential consequences and create a better future. If there is no emotional connection to the challenge, there is unlikely to be any motivation or energy to work with it now, or at a later stage.

Take some time to research further and ask:

- *So, what's the challenge you wish to work on?*
- *How is that a challenge for you? And for others?*
- *What is this preventing you from doing?*
- *What are the consequences of the challenge?*

You only need to get clients connected to the feelings and thoughts of the impact of the challenge briefly. Note down any emotionally charged phrases or 'hot words' they use that encapsulate the challenge for them. Pay attention to the client's physiology when in the challenge state. You can use these later in the session to test for change.

The next step is to 'break state' so the client can come out of the challenge state. In other words, it is important to change the topic and ensure that your client is now focused on something totally different from the challenge. *(Let's move to the next stage now and consider your outcome.)* Take responsibility for ensuring that they are at ease now. They should be breathing comfortably and not stuck in a negative or frustrated state.

Make it clear that this part is finished by 'outframing' the challenge, *I understand where we will be starting now. Let's park that challenge for a while.* This allows you to move cleanly on to eliciting outcomes.

Eliciting outcomes
Ask: *What is the outcome you wish to achieve?*

The aim of having an intention at this point is to establish a direction towards an outcome. This may however change and shift as the client becomes aware of new possibilities, insights and perceptions.

Establishing outcomes helps a client's unconscious mind to begin the work of looking for, anticipating and expecting something different. If the challenge was not having a motivated workforce or a team that does not communicate well (e.g. if working in silos), the outcome needs to be structured in the positive. It could be as general as:

- Find at least three ways (systems) to encourage all our teams to work together
- Define 'good communication' and get agreement from all our teams
- Establish steps to motivate teams and ways to test their effectiveness within the next six months.

Achieving outcomes
The outcome frame is very powerful. You can increase its potency naturally by asking for the evidence of success at the start. This will help the client focus more specifically on the outcome, what it will look like, and possible subsequent actions to achieve it.

- *How will you know you have achieved this outcome?*
- *What will you see, hear and feel that will let you know you have achieved it?*
- *What won't be happening that demonstrates progress has already been made?*
- *What are some of the visible and tangible signs that you are on track?*
- *Once you are making solid progress, how will you be feeling differently about the old challenge? What lets you know you are at that point now?*

Step 2: Explain the PMT process

At this point, explain the Physical Metaphor Technique. Give enough details about the initial step to get the client engaged. Tell them they will be creating a specific kind of scene: a diorama (three-dimensional 'metaphor' model) that represents the challenge, with objects that symbolise elements, themes and people within that scene. Using these objects they will move towards identifying a range of new options and strategies for achieving their outcome.

Use the environment
Ask the client to choose a physical space in the room within which they will work with their challenge. You may wish to suggest a space they can use, for example a desk top, table, rug or floor area. Let them know that this space is going to be special for the purposes of applying the PMT.

Once selected, invite the client to pick out a selection of different objects from around the room and bring them back to the chosen space. *Please look all around this room. Look everywhere. Look at your desk. Look inside the cupboards. Look inside your jacket pocket. Look inside your bag / purse / wallet. Pick out a selection of objects and bring them back to your chosen space.* You may also use Post-its and other paper to write on and place within the scene as well as, or instead of, objects.

The coach must never touch the objects or pick them up at any stage in the process. You can only refer to them. This is to ensure that the client retains full responsibility throughout the process and any decisions, or choices, that come from it. We want to communicate non-verbally, *This is your plan. You are resourceful and can generate new scenarios and possibilities based on this wider perspective.*

The essence of the PMT is to facilitate a process where the client is proactive, feels able to take full responsibility and is therefore empowered to try new things.

Step 3: Create establishing scene and ask orienting questions

Client creates establishing scene
Feed back a brief summary of the challenge from step #1 and ask the client to use any objects they have collected to create a representation of the challenge, thus creating the starting point for the scene.

- *Use any of these objects to create a scene that represents the challenge for you as you perceive it right now. Discard objects, or go and collect additional objects, at any time. There is no right or wrong way to do this. You decide what fits and what doesn't. This is your own creative space. Experiment with this initial scene until it feels right to you.*
- *I will be silent some of the time, and, at other times, I may ask questions about what is going on. Please let me know when it feels complete so that you can share the details of how the challenge looks in the scene.*

Ask orienting questions
Your aim at this point is to connect the client deeply to the symbolic meaning of the scene, so they feel totally invested in it and are able to explain why it has such meaning for them.

You want to leave them to reflect, especially if they are actively thinking and figuring things out as they construct the scene. Once they get into the exercise, it will take on a momentum of its own.

As the scene starts to come together and when the client signals it is complete, this may be a good time to ask any of the orienting questions below. Ask the client to describe the scene, what the objects represent to them and which are the most important or meaningful themes or items to them:

- *What does x represent?*
- *What attributes does y have?*
- *What is happening here? What else?*
- *How do you feel about that?*
- *What is the most important aspect of this? In what way?*
- Select and point to two objects in the scene and ask the client: *What is the relationship between x and y?*

A more in-depth explanation of metaphors and symbolism and their role in coaching can be found in Chapter 5: 'Coaching the Unconscious Mind through Metaphor' by Richard Haggerty.

Once you know a client is emotionally invested in this, and they have expressed the perceived parameters of the challenge, check to see if this scene is complete. *Is there anything else you would like to add to make this complete?* Once complete, let them know it is vitally important to capture the scene *before* they start working with it to achieve their outcome. They will then be able to assess progress later on and compare solutions against this initial scene. Photograph the scene now to record in their Coaching Report as a way to highlight the significance of what they have just created.

Step 4: Photograph establishing scene

Take a photo of the scene. A mobile phone or camera will suffice. You may want to have some Post-its that say 'scene

1' or 'scene 1: establishing scene,' so it is easy to identify the sequence later on, especially if you decide to include photos of all the intermediate steps.

Step 5: Move from challenge to outcome scene

Invite the client to create a new scene that begins to move them away from their challenge ('establishing scene') towards their outcome.

Remind the client of their overall outcome and ask some of the suggested questions below to help them get started:

- *So, what is your outcome?*
- *What do you want to have happen?*
- *What's the very first thing that needs to happen to move towards your outcome?*
- *What needs to happen next for this [establishing scene] to begin to change?*
- *If you wish to talk through your ideas please do so.*

Ask them to start making any changes e.g. move objects around, remove objects or add new ones to achieve their outcome. Invite them to take their time so that they fully process the significance of the moves and how they will work out in reality.

Stay curious about, and connected to, their process by being present, watchful and silent. Let your client sit longer in the silences, longer than we would all do 'normally.' The reason for this is that people think faster than they speak and the extra time in silence enables them to think more. Allow the client to be the one to initiate a conversation with you. When you do speak use *what* and *how* questions, rather than *why* or closed questions, and remain sensitive to the impact of your questioning. Remember this is *their* time and space and *never* give any interpretations of your own. Ask for theirs only. For example:

- *What will that move do for you?*
- *What is the significance of this?*
- *How will this support achieving your outcome?*

Listen deeply and attentively. Very quickly they will get the idea that they can experiment without consequence and judgement. The more space you create and the fewer words the coach says throughout the process, the more effective PMT is likely to be.

Ask follow-up questions
Now the client is creating a new 3D scene it is important to draw out the meaning behind the metaphors – or further metaphors – to solidify and further deepen any insights that are emerging spontaneously.

The more a client can articulate perceptions and own their observations, the more likely they are to develop confidence about influencing those perceptions.

Examples of open questions the coach can ask include:

- The outcome
  - o *What will the outcome look like relative to this scene?*
  - o *What has to change to continue towards the outcome?*
  - o *What else? What more?*
- *What is off limits here?*
- *What else is there that is not in the scene that you want to bring along now?*
- *What does this mean to you?*
- If the client seems stuck, or is having difficulty articulating at any point, then help them out: *I'm interested in what's happening here* [point to the part of the scene that you

are curious about]. *Tell me a bit more about this*, and finally,

- *What further steps do you want or need to take to achieve your outcome?* until the client indicates they have some ideas and strategies to resolve their challenge and to achieve their outcome.

Once the client indicates that the scene they have created is sufficiently transformed from the original problem-establishing scene, and, that they have a new range of options, strategies and potential new actions to move forward on, be sure to capture this.

You may also want to check that your client is at an outcome scene by asking: *How are you feeling now compared to the start of the session when you were sharing your challenge?* Raising awareness of how they are feeling now will also help convince them that some significant shifts and changes have already taken place throughout the session.

Step 6: Photograph final outcome scene

Photograph the scene as you did with the establishing scene. Remember it may be helpful to have a label or card to number / name the scene and date, so you know later what this represents and the sequence it comes in. You may want to take a few photos from different angles (e.g. from the side or from above).

By having an establishing scene and an outcome scene captured, it is possible to do a contrastive analysis: in other words, it will be far more obvious to note what needs to change, what relationships developed and what else needs to happen differently when a client can see where they have been and where they want to go.

Step 7: Agree actions and client dismantles scene

Throughout the 7 steps of the PMT, the client has been experiencing new ways of thinking about their challenge and possible solutions. It is important now to make these concrete by establishing specific next steps that they are committed to taking after the session.

At this point, you may ask the client to provide a brief summary of the actions and what they will be committing to do to move things forward. This may include:

- Recapping important insights
- Agreeing the actions to take to achieve the outcome
- Giving specific details of the next steps
- Including a way to assess the success of that action
- Committing to a specific date and time
- Ensuring the client is accountable for the above
- Asking them if there is anything else they wish to add.

Finally, it can be very useful to ask loaded, or leading questions with presuppositions of success in order to finish with a sense of mastery and leave the client recognising that something profound has occurred:

- *What was the most useful part of this for you?*
- *What insight do you feel will be the most helpful in making a change quickly?*
- *What resources do you have at your disposal already to begin to make this happen now?*

Inform the client that you will send their report to them within a specific period (e.g. three days).

Client dismantles the scene

The client needs closure – and to recognise the importance of what has just happened and their ownership of it – by taking this final step. Invite the client to dismantle the scene and put all the objects back in place. Remember, as coach, you *never* touch any part of the scene.

By putting everything back and dismantling the scene, there is a strong unconscious presupposition that the client is in charge of their thinking about the challenge and their ability to influence it. By creating their own physical metaphors, changing scenes and experimenting, they have demonstrated their ability to think (and act) outside the box.

This brings the PMT session to an end.

CASE STUDY

A regional CEO in the financial sector was having serious challenges: her large geographic region that stretched across several countries was not meeting its numbers; her leadership team was ground down by the continuing pressures to turn around their performance within a highly competitive market; her boss was under pressure to deliver and felt his job was on the line; and the regional CEO was almost at a loss as to how to catapult the business into being a success where others had previously failed. The world was on her back and her posture showed it.

She requested some coaching to support her developing different ways of thinking about the challenges and identifying practical, new or different solutions to move towards turning the business around.

She explained to me that although she had engaged her boss, her peers and her team members to gain their insights and perspectives, the outputs were not far reaching enough to make the difference that was now imperative. She was stuck in her present way of thinking.

On the first day, knowing that she wanted a different approach, I invited her to use the meeting room as a landscape for the problems she was facing and to place and rearrange objects in the room (large or small, tables and chairs included) to show the nature of the problem she was facing. The team became the chairs, the regional countries became the table and her boss became a large heavy sculpture in the corner of the door. Then we got into the detail.

As her coach I invited her to consider the following questions to support her new thinking:

- *Who are the other key people and organisations who are part of the scenario?*
- *Who are the key competitors?*
- *Who are not competitors, though key influencers in the region?*
- *Who do you know (a friend or ex colleague) that has significantly different views from you and can challenge you to think 'outside the box'?*
- *What would they ask you? Suggest to you?*
- *What would they do in your position? What stops you from doing that too? How could you do a variation of that?*

As we continued with these types of questions, she was constantly moving around the room, moving objects around the room, and talking out loud about the different possibilities this type of questioning and technique was triggering in her.

She was excited. She was starting to become aware of new choices she could make and options available to her.

Within the hour she decided that she had sufficient ideas to discuss with her key stakeholders and gain their inputs, ideas and support for these.

We followed this with one further session to take her thinking to the next stage, and another one to work on building her own identity as a leader and reinforce the huge strengths and talents she had and the confidence this gave her, something she had forgotten over so many recent years of challenges and missed targets.

The result was that she discovered some ingenious ways forward that all employees within the region became a part of. She was on a mission! Together, with the huge efforts from all the teams across the region, they achieved a giant leap in business performance and went beyond their targets.

For a more in-depth look at techniques to work with and leverage one's identity go to Chapter 10: 'Coaching for Identity Grows Purpose and Performance' by Aidan Tod.

Coaching insights and summary

The Physical Metaphor Technique (PMT) technique is a powerful and systematic way to externalise the challenge that your client is exploring as physical mutable metaphors that they control. This tends to increase their confidence and willingness to test and explore solutions, whilst gaining the necessary perspectives to leave behind any negative or unhelpful thinking that may have kept them stuck.

Although this technique is developed along the lines of military war games, it can also be used with groups of individuals for business, or corporate war gaming. In this way, leaders and decision-makers can come together and 'shape the battlefield' by creating the competitive landscape and playing out (simulating) a range of potential scenarios and decide on the best prospects for their businesses. Whichever sector your clients work in, no one really knows what next year's 'trends' will be. However it is the smarter ones who take the time to 'mould the space' and create next year's 'trend,' and who lead in their fields.[1]

~

Connect with the Authors
We hope you enjoyed reading about this experiential hands-on technique that can be used with individual clients, or indeed with small teams of leaders, who seek to identify new ways forward. To find out more, to connect with us or to explore further creative methods for generating sustainable behavioural change in your clients and their businesses, please contact Veronica Munro at results@veronicamunro.com and at www.veronicamunro.com or Richard Haggerty at richard@richardhaggerty.co.uk and at www.richardhaggerty.co.uk

---

1   After we had written this chapter, it was brought to our attention that Gestalt coaching uses a similar approach in the context of coaching and coaching supervision and was named 'The Magic Box' by Edna Murdoch in 2001.

CHAPTER 2

TAKE THE PLUNGE AND DIVE DEEPER USING TRANSACTIONAL ANALYSIS

Shirley Attenborough

Transactional Analysis (TA) is a tool that provides a rich and stimulating explanation of our social relationships and why we behave the way we do. It suggests that aspects of our personality are formed in early childhood. Once we are aware of this, we can work towards adapting our behaviour to have more successful interactions.

Covered in this chapter

- A roadmap to help understand the default ways we communicate with others, and likely consequences
- The different Ego States and the behaviours associated with each
- Explanation of the tools that can be useful in changing behaviour
- Case studies providing examples of how the above are achieved

---

INTRODUCING THE TOOLS

Transactional Analysis (TA) is a simple, empowering way to assist clients to step out of their comfort zone, and to explore the way they interact, transact, and communicate. The tool supports clients to take the plunge, breathe deeply and understand what is going on deep inside themselves. TA also assists us to become more aware about the way we communicate as coaches. It can support us to decide how to behave differently in order to get a more successful result.

TA facilitates easy and immediate reflection, as well as enabling us to step back and see issues from different perspectives. It provides valuable feedback about our interactions, allows us to reflect both during and after a coaching session, and enables us to try out different ways of communicating in a safe environment.

This chapter provides structural and functional diagrams to support your understanding, together with a variety of case studies to demonstrate how the theory plays out in practice, and how easily and simply it can be applied.

For those who want a concrete definition, the one provided by the dictionary (dictionary.com) is clearest:

> a system of popular psychology based on the idea that one's behaviour and social relationships reflect an interchange between parental (critical and nurturing), adult (rational) and childlike (intuitive and dependent) aspects of personality established early in life.

Playing games: background to TA

Eric Berne, the founder of TA, wrote *Games People Play* (1964), which became a bestseller and, since its publication, has sold more than five million copies, and put TA firmly on the transformation map. Berne, a psychiatrist, developed TA for therapeutic and counselling settings, and subsequently it is being used in organisations. He described TA as a system of psychology to understand, predict, and change behaviour.

As a psychiatrist, Berne came from the premise that people need fixing. In coaching, we operate from the presupposition that people are whole and do not need fixing, and are able to work out what they need for themselves. The TA model has been adapted to fit the coaching model so it works in organisations.

We start with a description of the Ego States Model, followed by the Life Position / OK Corral model. We will discover how we can use these two models together to support clients to understand their behaviour, and to explore ways of changing these, if they want to. TA at its fullest is a complex and demanding topic. This chapter is an introduction to TA that works in harmony with many different coaching approaches.

To begin, we need to get a clear picture of the structure and function of this theoretical model. (All diagrams within this chapter are commonly used to describe and explain Eric Berne's work and, latterly, Ernst's OK Corral.)

BASIC FUNCTION OF THE EGO STATES MODEL

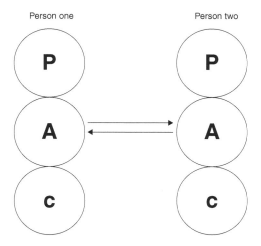

Figure 2.1: The Ego States Model

The first circle represents the Parent Ego State. The second circle represents the Integrated Adult Ego State. The third circle represents the Child Ego State.

Throughout this chapter it is important to remember to avoid confusing the Parent, Adult, and Child Ego States with being an 'actual' parent, adult or child. The Ego States are labels to help us identify and give a name to how we are behaving at a particular moment!

It is also important to note that engaging with the conscious mind is the beginning of our journey within. TA is particularly effective when working with people because it gives them a way to reflect on automatic behaviours, patterns and emotions without feeling defensive, vulnerable or challenged – to the extent that they can gain insight through their own observations.

When you start a session with a client, draw the above six circles on a piece of paper and label them, ready for discussion.

CASE STUDY 1: NOT 'SHOWING UP' IN MEETINGS

A successful banker was being considered for promotion. He had been informed by his boss and the review panel that he needed to 'show up' more in meetings, especially virtual meetings across different regions. I asked my client what this meant. He explained that he had no problem sharing his views with peers in the office, but he was uncomfortable when he thought he might be upsetting or ruffling the feathers of senior colleagues or colleagues he didn't know well. My client thought it was important to be liked by people. I asked if he would like to explore this in more depth, and he agreed. We both drew the model, and the conversation developed as below.

I asked, *How do you identify with the different Ego States?* After a pause, he described situations when young; he was not expected to speak, comment or have an opinion in front of his elders, or those considered more important than him. My client recognised that in some situations he was still behaving this way. He was clearly surprised, and quite reflective. He commented that this had to change as it was preventing him from reaching his full potential. We talked about this, and I asked: *What does change mean to you?*

He spent a long time working his way around the model. He identified that there were many times at work when he was communicating from the Adult Ego State, and other times when he was operating from the Child Ego State.

We spent time exploring what he wanted to do differently, what needed to happen to help him, and how he was going to manage himself when he was with certain people. He felt that some of his behaviour was so ingrained from his childhood that it was going to take time and practice. He noted that colleagues around him from similar backgrounds had adopted the Parent Ego State. This was something he was keen to avoid, and he felt that his new self-awareness was a start in moving into the Integrated Adult Ego State. The goal of TA is to assist people in communicating Adult to Adult.

Berne explains that we all have three Ego States, and that we use all three to communicate. However, only one is active at any given time. Although we move through all the States all the time, we are not necessarily in the same Ego State as the person we are communicating with. This is often where problems start! We are sometimes in what Berne referred to as 'complementary' Ego States. These are Adult to Adult, Parent to Child and Child to Parent, or Child to Child and Parent to Parent.

COMPLEMENTARY EGO STATES

Adult to Adult

When we are operating from the Adult Ego State, we are in the 'here and now,' and our interactions are logical, rational, and without contamination from previous experience. The goal of TA is to assist people to spend more time communicating from Adult to Adult. An interaction would look something like this:

Person One (Adult): 'I'm really struggling with this work. Can you help?'

Person Two (Adult): 'Yes of course. What would you like me to do?'

Parent to Child and Child to Parent

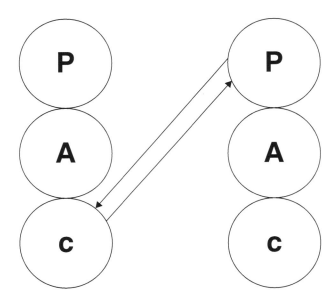

Figure 2.2: Different Ego States

A different scenario when we are not communicating so effectively occurs when the parties involved are in different Ego States. For example, when a transaction begins with someone operating from the Parent Ego State, which is often received by the recipient as an invitation to respond from the Child Ego State and vice versa. An interaction would probably look something like this.

Parent to Child:
Person One (Parent) angrily says 'I asked you for that work ages ago. Haven't you done it yet?'

Person Two (Child) whining 'I've been trying but it's really hard. Why are you always yelling at me?'

Child to Parent:
Person One (Child) says frustratedly, 'This is too difficult. I can't do it'

Person Two (Parent) frustratedly says 'I have showed you how to do it so many times. What's wrong with you?'

The above illustrates how we operate from a Parent Ego State, and receive a response from the Child Ego State or vice versa. It is rarely effective communication.

The other two complementary Ego States are Child to Child and Parent to Parent. These types of transaction are also unlikely to encourage mature, appropriate conversations.

Crossed Ego States

At other times we could be communicating in 'crossed' Ego States.

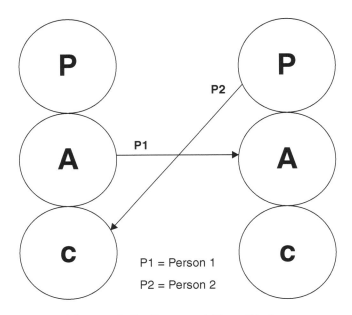

Figure 2.3: Crossed Ego States

A crossed Ego State occurs when one person (P1) invites another for an 'Adult' response to an 'Adult' request. Instead of responding from Adult, the other person (P2) responds from either the Parent or Child Ego State. Then the exchange between two colleagues might look like this:

Colleague one (Adult) 'Do you know where X file is?'

Colleague two (Parent) replies angrily, 'For goodness sake, you are always losing it. It is where you left it.'

If you refer back to the diagram, colleague one asked a question from Adult, and invited an Adult response, the location of the file. Instead his colleague responded from a Parent Ego State, so the communication became crossed. Probably at this stage colleague one is likely to respond back from the Child Ego State, and the conversation can continue in an unsatisfactory way until one of them invites the other into an Adult response. This is, of course, where mature, in-the-moment conversations happen.

USING TA AND EGO STATES IN THE WORKPLACE

As previously mentioned, TA was initially a counselling tool, and has only recently been used more widely in the business context, though there are differences in terms of its application in the workplace. Berne originally proposed four separate scenarios for assessing which Ego State an individual is possibly operating in at a particular moment.

The four areas are:

1. **Behavioural:** observing posture, gestures, language, tone, and tempo of speech.

2. **Social assessment:** observing an interaction between two people and their behaviour.

3. **Historical:** when we are in the Child Ego State, we are 'feeling' as adults the behaviour, feelings and emotions that we experienced as children. In a work environment, and normally in coaching, we wouldn't ask!

4. **Phenomenological assessment:** is not just about *feeling* a past event, but actually *re-experiencing* it and would be inappropriate in the coaching environment.

It is only appropriate to use 1. Behavioural and 2. Social assessment whilst coaching in the workplace. TA practitioners have suggested that the Ego States Model should be used in conjunction with a second framework, referred to as the Life Positions quadrant, or, more fondly, as the OK Corral.

Let us look at how the Ego States are further divided, and their associated behaviours. These can be used to provide clients with clues about their own behaviour, thoughts and feelings. Ego States are internal, but they are manifested in our behaviour. By asking questions, we can understand what emotions and feelings accompany these different behaviours. After that, we can take a closer look at the Life Positions OK Corral model.

EGO STATES AND THEIR ASSOCIATED BEHAVIOURS

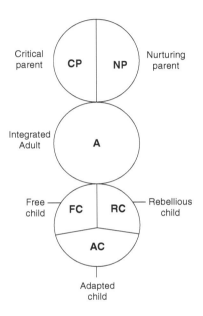

Figure 2.4: Associated behaviours

Parent State

When we are in the Parent Ego State, we think, feel and behave in ways based on parent and authority figures we observed growing up. This is divided into Critical or Controlling Parent on the left, and Nurturing Parent on the right. Both of these Ego States have positive and negative behaviours, also referred to as OK (positive) and Not OK (negative).

Starting with the left: Critical / Controlling Parent. The behaviours are positive when they come from a place that doesn't undermine us. An example might be that the parent organises a bedtime at 7 pm in order for the child to get up and be fresh in the morning for school, whereas a negative behaviour is used to undermine us. For example, you are asked to wash up and then you are told, 'Give me the dish cloth. You can't do anything right, you are so stupid.' A Controlling Parent can come from a positive place in terms of giving us social norms to live by, or a negative place when the comment is designed to undermine us.

Let's take a moment and think about how a Controlling Parent's behaviour might play out in the office. A boss figure might single out an individual in the team meeting, and make a detrimental comment about a report they have written.

Similarly, a Nurturing Parent can be positive and OK, for example, when they tuck us in at night, and tell a bedtime story. However, if the behaviour becomes smothering or invasive, it becomes negative and Not OK. For example, 'Please don't ever run as you might fall over.' This behaviour is over-protective as it doesn't allow us to grow, and become independent capable people. Nurturing Parent may play out in the office in a more subtle fashion such as an employee handing in a report to their boss, who then corrects, changes and circulates it without consulting them. This over-protective boss isn't helping them to grow or develop their skills, even though they might think that their behaviour is coming from a 'good' place.

Positive behaviour could be when a boss takes the employee to one side to discuss the report, and then asks: What is good about the report? What works well? What doesn't work so well? What could they do / write differently? Following this, the boss could offer what they thought had been done well, and then add 'and it would be even better if "x" had been included.' In this way, they are making suggestions for their employee's development and improvement that doesn't undermine and demotivate.

Adult Ego State

The second circle is the Integrated Adult Ego State. As previously mentioned, this only has positive behaviours and is 'OK.' When we are responding from here, our behaviour comes from the 'here and now,' is non-judgemental, and not contaminated by previous experience. We are therefore responding maturely, rationally and appropriately in the situation.

Child Ego State

The third circle is the Child Ego States. When we are in one of the three Child Ego States we are replaying and remembering how we behaved during childhood. Again, these three Ego States contain positive or OK behaviours, and negative Not OK behaviours. When in the positive or OK Free Child Ego State, the behaviour is all about creativity and playfulness. When Free Child is negative or Not OK, the behaviour is inconsiderate, wild and uncontrolled.

The Rebellious Child Ego State behaviour, where positive and OK, is about high achievement both professionally and personally. These behaviours include overcoming difficult, challenging goals, persistence and determination as well as enjoying positions of power. The negative or Not OK behaviours include demanding attention and energy from others, being aggressively sarcastic, blaming and judgemental.

Finally, when in an Adapted Child Ego State, the positive OK behaviours include accommodating others, and being co-operative. The negative and Not OK behaviours include being over-compliant, passive aggressive or defiant and difficult. An example might be agreeing to take on extra work when we don't want to, or alternatively, saying we will do something, but don't!

If we pause here and reflect, we can probably recognise many of the above behaviours in ourselves and others, both inside, and outside the work place.

We have mentioned OK and Not OK behaviour in terms of positive and negative behaviours associated with the Ego States Model. Now it is time to explore our second model: Life Positions / OK Corral. This second model is very useful for helping individuals to understand how they might consciously or unconsciously be viewing themselves and others through their behaviour. We may consciously and unconsciously see ourselves as OK or Not OK. We may view others in the same way, or a combination of OK and Not OK.

FRANCK ERNST OK CORRAL / LIFE POSITIONS

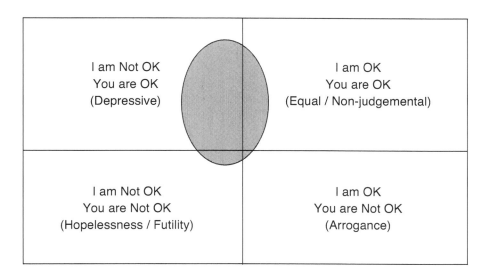

Figure 2.5: OK Corral / Life Positions

This theory suggests that we use all of the four Life Positions in different situations and with different people. However, we will each have a preferred Life Position based upon early experience.

In the quadrant above, if the person's Life Position is more in the top left quadrant: 'I am not OK, you are OK,' this can be expressed as feeling less worthy than someone else. The opposite of this would be when someone's Life Position is predominantly in the bottom right quadrant: 'I am OK, you are Not OK,' which can be expressed as feeling better than others.

Practical application

We can use this tool in different ways and at different points in a coaching session, or block of coaching sessions. In order to be most effective, these tools really benefit the client after several coaching sessions and once trust has been established with the coach. Life Positions, put simply, are our perceptions of the world and our place in it. It is not reality, but only how we perceive our reality to be as individuals. We also move around the different Life Positions depending upon the situation and the people around us.

Developing increased self-awareness

We each have a preferred or predominant Life Position and this position is decided early in our lives. However, from a coaching perspective how we arrived at the Life Position is less important than where we are today, and where we want to be going forward. If our clients are open to exploring their possible Life Positions, it can provide them with a lot of information about themselves, help them to increase their self-awareness, and understand their own behaviour, as well as how they communicate. A client has to be ready and want to have this experience. We should only move forward after we have offered an invitation to the client, and they are ready to dive deeper and explore further.

Exploration

Another way to use the model, which initially may be less intimidating, is when a client is describing a recent interaction. We can invite them to use the OK Corral to explore where on the quadrant they, and the person they were interacting with, appear to be operating from. Remember we can't verify any information. This is just an exploration to assist our clients to enhance their self-awareness. Then, using a gentle questioning technique, we are able to support them to explore these in more depth and detail.

Diving deeply

Clients can begin to reflect at a deeper level, and to explore what is going on in their conscious thinking, and deeper into their heart and body. They can explore their feelings and emotions more deeply in order to understand more fully and appreciate their triggers, responses and behaviours. They may identify some automatic behaviours that were completely outside their conscious awareness. They might want to consider how well their current behaviours in certain situations, or around specific people, are working or not working.

- *What is the ripple effect their behaviour might be having across their different relationships and across the organisation?*

- *What would they like to change?*
- *What benefits would behaviour change bring to themselves and others?*

How the OK Corral relates to the Ego States Model

In the top left quadrant, 'I am Not OK, You are OK,' we can see how this might relate to the negative Adapted Child Ego State. The top right, 'I am OK, You are OK' would fit well with Adult Ego State, a position of awareness and equals, without judgement. This is where we would all like to be when we are communicating well, and operating at our very best.

If we look at the lower right quadrant, 'I am OK, You are Not OK,' the overall message here is one of arrogance. This suggests the Parent negative Ego State of either Critical or Nurturing Parent. The suggestion here is that the other person is doing something wrong and / or is incompetent.

Finally, in the bottom left quadrant, 'I am Not OK, You are Not OK,' is clearly a position of hopelessness and / or futility for both. So again, the negatives associated with a Child Ego State would fit here.

Now we have looked at the basics of these two models let's reflect on ourselves, the different people we engage with and the situations we find ourselves in. How well do you communicate? Which of the Ego States do you notice yourself operating from?

The model works equally well in a variety of coaching scenarios including face to face, over the telephone, video conferencing and with groups. Here are some further everyday examples that people can relate to.

CASE STUDY 2: OVER-REACTION

A client shared a series of incidents she had experienced in which she began to feel that she was over-reacting. She realised that she wasn't doing herself any favours in terms of her future career or building relationships in her network. She described the latest incident. She had received an email from a colleague and although the email wasn't rude, she felt unappreciated. She had sent an email back, copying in a lot of other colleagues, saying she didn't want to receive such emails again.

I asked her what she would do now if she received a similar email, and she said she would do it again. I asked, *Even though you have said you shouldn't, you still would?* She replied 'Yes!' I said, *Can you think of other times when you have done this?* Again, she said 'Yes.' I asked her what was going on, what were her feelings, and what was she thinking at those times? What triggered those incidents? She said it was always about when she was feeling unappreciated and undervalued. I asked if there were specific times she could recall. She immediately described a teacher at school who had unjustly criticised her and undervalued her contribution. At the time, she was unable to respond. She went on to say that she still wanted to go back and find the teacher and tell them how she had felt.

I asked if she was willing to explore a model with me. I drew out and described both the Ego States Model and the OK Corral. I asked her which quadrant she thought she might be in when this was happening? She immediately said, 'I'm OK, You are Not OK.' She said that she felt unappreciated. Her response was to share with everyone that she was OK, and that the other person wasn't. She added that in retrospect what she was actually doing was sharing that she wasn't OK, and the other person wasn't OK either.

I asked which Ego State she might be operating from, and she laughed and said possibly Adapted or Rebellious Child. I asked her what she would do now if she found herself in a similar position. She replied, 'I would still take it back to the person, but in private and less aggressively.'

We continued to discuss the issue from different perspectives, and she commented that she had enjoyed working with the model. It made it easy for her to think about how she sometimes responds automatically, and hopefully over time and with practice, she would respond differently, in order to get a more effective and helpful response.

She also commented that by looking at a model on paper, she was able to think about herself in different situations, without becoming emotional or defensive. I asked her what not becoming emotional or too defensive meant? She replied that she felt she judged herself less harshly, and this enabled her to explore in a safe way. In future sessions, we used the model to take some much deeper dives into her thinking, feeling and behaviours.

To discover more coaching tools to change the way you think, and your clients' thinking, see Chapter 4: 'Breaking Free: Unlocking Doors with Deep Reframing' by Richard Haggerty.

CASE STUDY 3: FEELING UNDERMINED

This client was struggling with his new boss. Previously they had been colleagues and peers. My client hadn't applied for the position as boss, so there was no animosity regarding that. He really couldn't understand what was going wrong, and said, 'I just feel undermined all the time.' He couldn't put a finger on what was going on but he had stopped enjoying work, and had begun to look for another job.

We explored his current set up, and then I asked if he remembered feeling like this before, and if so, who did it remind him of? He thought for a while, and said, 'Yes, it's how I felt around my father sometimes.' I could see that the Ego States and Life Position Models might be helpful for my client. He accepted my offer to explore, and quickly identified with the model on several different levels. He felt he was being spoken to from Critical Parent, and he thought it had something to do with the tone of voice. He also recognised that he was responding from the Child Ego State.

We continued to explore this in terms of which quadrant in the OK Corral he was in. The most immediate effect for him was relief that he could identify what was going on. He also said that his relationship with his new boss was a good one, and now that he understood what was going on, he was going to have an open discussion with him. He said that he felt that he would find it relatively easy to communicate with his boss from the Adult Ego State and the 'I am OK, You are OK' quadrant now that he understood himself better. This was just the starting point of us using the model together. Over subsequent sessions, he explored his style of communication and became more and more comfortable taking deeper and deeper dives.

CASE STUDY 4: STRUGGLING TO WORK WITH A COLLEAGUE (AND DIDN'T KNOW WHY)

Another client was struggling to work with a colleague during working hours. When they were out socially the same didn't apply, and they communicated really well. I suggested working with a couple of models, and she readily agreed. She quickly identified that she was in the 'I'm Not OK, You are Not OK' quadrant. She also recognised that she was operating from a Rebellious Child Ego State. There was a light-bulb moment when she realised that when they were at work, she felt that her colleague was judging her, telling her how to complete certain tasks. She also recognised that she meant well, but this didn't stop her from feeling angry and put out.

She had another insightful moment when she recognised her colleague's behaviour as negative Nurturing Parent, and that her own mother had behaved in a similar way when she was growing up. She spent some time reflecting on this information. She visibly relaxed and smiled and said that she now understood what was annoying her, and it wouldn't any more. She thought that she could move easily into the 'I am OK, You are OK' quadrant. She had a new perspective, and now felt supported by her colleague.

CASE STUDY 5: DOESN'T SUFFER FOOLS GLADLY

A very successful Chief Operating Officer (COO) is highly practical and in his own words 'doesn't suffer fools gladly.' He was finding that although he was very successful, others in the organisation were complaining about his communication style (abrupt, rude and arrogant). He had decided that he wanted to explore this but wasn't sure if he wanted to change his behaviour, as he saw the issues and problems as belonging to someone else. I worked with this client on the telephone. After a few sessions, I asked him if he was willing to explore a theoretical model, and he agreed.

I started by asking him to draw the three circles and simply label them Parent, Adult, and Child. Before I had a chance to say anything else, he said, 'You are calling me a child!' I laughed and said *Really? Am I? What makes you think that? I only asked you to draw three circles in a vertical line and give them each a label.* He was quiet for a few moments and I stayed quiet. Then he said, 'I think you asked me to draw this because you think I behave like a child.' I continued to stay quiet, and then after a while I said, *Can we explore the model a little without judgement from either of us?* He agreed, and discussion about the model followed.

He then stated, 'Yes, I can see that I could be described as behaving as either a Rebellious Child or a Controlling Parent.' At this point he was in the 'Not OK' position, but very quickly went on to say how frustrated he was with certain others. He blamed them for the way he spoke to them. He had moved to the 'I am OK, You are Not OK' position.

After more exploration and more questions, he also realised that the way he behaved with them wasn't getting him what he wanted. He further commented that he wanted to be perceived as an ambassador for the organisation, and in order to achieve that, he needed to express himself more engagingly.

He often used humour to explore difficult conversations he was having with different colleagues, and he could laugh at himself. Although he didn't change his communication style overnight, he did discuss wanting to spend more time in the top right quadrant 'I am OK, You are OK.' He also commented that he liked this new way of looking at himself and at others.

As our sessions continued, he told me that although he was still frustrated with certain people, and behaved in the same way as before, there were times when he paused and planned his conversations. He further noted that it wasn't always easy to change, and that sometimes it was only after an interaction that he stopped to think. He commented that he had gone to his preferred Life Position which he identified as 'I am OK, You are Not OK.' He added that he didn't care about getting different responses but he did care about being perceived as an ambassador at certain times. He therefore only occasionally changed his behaviours when in front of selected people.

What he liked about these models was that he had increased his awareness, and that he now had a clear choice about how to communicate. He also added mischievously that there were some people who frustrated him so much that he wanted them to be aware of his frustration, and that he didn't believe that some deserved the effort it would take for him to change.

It is important to note that, although coaching increases self-awareness and choices for clients, it is up to them to determine how far that change will go and the extent to which they wish to modify their behaviours.

To further investigate the domain of emotions, see Dan Newby's two chapters on emotions in Part III: 'The Heart of the Matter: A New Interpretation of Emotions' and 'Getting to the Heart of the Matter: Emotions-Centred Coaching.'

Coaching insights and summary

When clients are focusing on the models, they are less self-conscious, more relaxed, and each time they use them they feel more comfortable to take deeper dives and explore the challenges they have.

TA used in a coaching context also provides the coach with a powerful opportunity for increased self-awareness whilst reflecting on coaching sessions. The models can help the coach think about what could have been done differently that might have supported the clients even more effectively, thus providing further learning for the coach and improvement of future coaching sessions.

The TA tools can support a powerful way for the client to be present and help them to disassociate long enough to gain new perspectives. By gently nudging them to tell you which quadrant or which Ego State they are in, in a given situation, you simply and non-judgementally stay curious and interested, and ask questions.

~

Connect with the Author
So, are you ready to take the plunge and dive deeply with your own coaching practice? I really hope so, and if you have any questions or feedback, I would be delighted to hear from you at shirleyattenborough@gmail.com

References

Eric Berne, *Games people play: the psychology of human relationships* (Ballantine Books, 1964)

Eric Berne, *What do you say after you say hello* (André Deutsch, 1972)

Franklin H. Ernst Jr., *Transactional Analysis J.* 1:4 October (1971)

Richard Erskine, *Relational patterns, therapeutic presence: concepts and practice of integrative psychology* (Kanac Books, 2015)

Thomas Harris, *I'm OK you're OK* (Avon Books, 1966)

Anita Mountain and Chris Davidson, *Working together* (Gower, 2011)

Ian Stewart and Vann Joines, *TA today* (Lifespace Publishing, 2012)

CHAPTER 3

THE TRANSFORMATIONAL IMPACT OF ACTIVE LISTENING

Colin D. Smith

Active Listening is widely acknowledged by top leaders and coaches as being fundamental to their business and personal success. It is a skill that can be learned and embodied into the way we lead, manage and coach. When our clients, colleagues and employees feel deeply heard, they will be more willing to share their deepest challenges, needs and concerns. As a result, the business will gain more engaged, motivated and higher performing individuals and teams, transforming into improved results.

Covered in this chapter

- How the Relationship Journey builds trust, engagement and stronger personal relationships with your peers, employees, clients and suppliers, and especially those closest to you
- The 7 steps on how to actively listen to your clients
- The difference between hearing and listening
- How trust is built step by step
- How to create a safe place and how to use it with good intention
- The 12 elements of Active Listening
- The value of appreciation
- Simple Active Listening tips and exercises to include in your practice

---

INTRODUCTION

Why Active Listening?

Why is Active Listening so important, and why this chapter? Active Listening is at the heart of achieving transformational change with our coaching clients, as well as being the foundation of all our relationships, both at work and personally. A coach who is able to listen effectively builds deep levels of rapport and presence with a client and is able to tease out and work with the deeper elements that make sustainable change possible. These include a client's beliefs, values, emotions, ways of being, and identity.

The journey within, therefore, begins with focusing one's conscious attention sufficiently to be able to have a meaningful conversation. The key to this is to build trust through listening and holding a clear positive intention.

Active Listening is vital and life changing and is the starting point for:

- Developing more meaningful relationships
- Building deeper connections with your clients
- Enabling clients to express themselves more freely
- Giving clients space and time for more creative and original thinking
- Supporting clients to experience greater self-awareness, confidence and presence.

We are not trained to listen

We listen more than any other mode of communication. We listen 45% of the time compared to writing 9%, reading 16%, and speaking 30%. Yet we have little or no formal training in listening, that is, how to listen effectively, what to listen for, and the benefits of listening in business and in our everyday relationships.

We speak and think at different speeds

We speak at around 125 words per minute (wpm), yet we can think at around 450 wpm. This means that for the listener, we have the capacity to hear everything the speaker is saying and have the bandwidth to think of many other things. This is one of the reasons we listen so poorly: we get distracted.

For the speaker, they too are thinking at 450 wpm, yet can only speak their words at 125 wpm, which means their first words spoken are most likely to be from the top of their mind. If the speaker is able to pause and not be interrupted they will continue speaking. It is only then that their words will come from a deeper part of their thinking.

Listening does not mean counselling

Listening has always had a big part to play in counselling and psychotherapy. In business, however, listening is more often seen as a 'soft skill,' a 'nice to have' or even something to quietly smile about to ourselves. After all, where is the profit in listening?

It is, however, becoming increasingly accepted that listening is a crucial skill for everyone, especially leaders and coaches.

By adding listening to your repertoire of skills, you will notice how it profoundly affects all those around you. When they feel heard, you will notice their increased attention, openness and willingness to bring their best thinking to meetings where previously they had remained quiet.

Furthermore, as people feel more open and willing to share their feelings and concerns, the impact is felt across the business, e.g. projects run on time and within budget, safety issues and concerns are raised earlier, new ideas are more frequent, creativity and innovation are increased, and open sharing becomes the way.

Overall, you will notice an improvement in individual and team performance.

Research highlights the importance of listening

The global sales training company, Huthwaite, completed an international survey in 2016 that identified customers' attitudes towards sales teams and what they considered most important. Listening scored 73%, second only to product knowledge at 79%.[1]

A recent CFA (Chartered Financial Analysts) survey also showed that the most useful consulting skill was listening 54%, followed by presenting at 15%.[2]

When was the last time you felt really listened to?

For many people, this is not an easy question to answer. In considering our answer, we run through the many and varied conversations that we have had, and we suddenly realise that most of the time we didn't really feel heard or understood.

---

1   'The sales skills that will get you hired (or promoted) in 2016,' *Salesforce blog*, 23 December 2015, www.salesforce.com/ca/blog/2015/12/sales-skills-2016.html

2   'Listen up: communication skills and your career,' *Enterprising Investor*, 10 March 2016, https://blogs.cfainstitute.org/investor/2016/03/10/listen-up-communication-skills-and-your-career

As we think more deeply, we are only able to find one or two occasions where we did feel heard, and, typically, it evokes a positive feeling within us.

In asking a group, 'Raise your arm if you believe you are a better than average listener?' usually, everyone raises their arm. When then asked, 'Keep your arm raised if anyone has said, "Thank you for listening", in the last two weeks.' The majority will take them down.

Hearing or listening?

Let's look at the meaning of hearing and why it is fundamentally different from listening.

- '*We hear from*': we don't have to do anything to hear the speaker. Hearing is passive. It is an ability the majority of us have and happens without our needing to think. For example, if someone calls your name out across a noisy room, you will hear it. If a train passes whilst you are sleeping, you will hear it, until you get used to it. Hearing, primarily, keeps us safe.
- '*We listen to*': we have to choose to listen to the person speaking. Listening is active and participative, yet it looks like you are doing nothing. We don't talk over people, we don't interrupt, we don't finish off the speaker's sentences. Instead we patiently allow people to finish what they wish to say and we ask questions and summarise what they say to ensure we understand them. This clearly demonstrates to the speaker they are being heard.

When a speaker feels they are being heard, they are more likely to like and trust the person listening.

THE RELATIONSHIP JOURNEY

The Relationship Journey is a series of steps, along with the ongoing awareness of the intention we are holding throughout the journey. These steps apply whether the relationship is professional or personal.

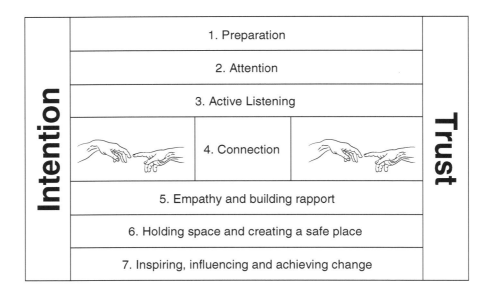

Figure 3.1: The Relationship Journey

Intention

In Figure 3.1, intention is shown alongside the steps on the Relationship Journey because it is present at all times. Intention is a conscious choice and may be unseen and unheard. In the context of coaching, however, it is important to let your client know your intention, honestly and clearly, at each stage of the coaching and precisely what is expected of them, as this will facilitate building a trusting and effective relationship between you. This, in turn, facilitates more effective outcomes from the coaching as there will be more openness and less resistance from the client.

Trust

On the right-hand side of the Relationship Journey is trust. Building trust is important for leaders and coaches. It can take time to achieve this, and yet it can be broken in an instant through lack of attention, or through focusing on what we want and not on the needs of the client. Perhaps too there may be a need to get results quickly and therefore some people inadvertently rush through the stages of the relationship before rapport is truly built.

Great leaders, as well as great coaches, who create high levels of followership, are known to be experts at engaging with others and actively listening to them. In this way, they build highly effective trusting relationships and hence followership.

For further information, see Chapter 2: 'Take the Plunge and Dive Deeper using Transactional Analysis' by Shirley Attenborough, in which she references the Adult Ego State and its relation to non-judgement.

THE RELATIONSHIP JOURNEY: THE 7 STEPS

1. Preparation: understanding the logistics

Top performers would not dream of just 'turning up' to an event or a job interview, hoping to be successful by just 'winging' it. Yet many of us are so time pressured that sometimes we just 'turn up' with insufficient preparation.

Whatever the situation, before you arrive, consider

- *Your audience*: is it one-to-one, a board, a team, or a large group?
- What is your outcome and purpose of the meeting?
- *The conversation*: is it formal, informal, feedback, or learning?
- *The location*: clients need the space to relax and feel comfortable, safe and secure. Does the space show that they matter to you and that you care?
- *The environment*: is it appropriate for the conversation, could there be interruptions, could it be too noisy, too quiet, and will it be suitable if emotions arise?
- *The style*: sitting, standing or walking whilst talking and listening?
- What else might be required by the client or those in the meeting?

2. Attention

Giving your full attention is probably the greatest gift you can give to someone.

Although attention is something we can all do really well, many of us have forgotten how, been conditioned out of, or are too busy, to do. Remembering or re-learning can have a positive impact on the quality of your relationships.

Can you remember how you felt when someone gave you their full attention?

And when they didn't … you knew.

The 7 simple steps to giving attention

1. Be clear on your positive intention for your client
2. Make eye contact, a soft gaze not a stare
3. Relax and breathe. Tip: relax your forehead and any tension around your eyes
4. Keep your body open and relaxed, arms and legs uncrossed
5. Physically lean slightly towards the speaker where appropriate
6. Be aware that this time is for them
7. For this moment, have in your mind that they are the most important person in your life.

3. Active Listening: the 12 elements

Active Listening is the key step in the Relationship Journey. Each of the 12 elements is stand-alone and can be practised on its own. As you use them, you will quickly notice the impact Active Listening has on the way a client or colleague responds to you.

Use the checklist below to train yourself to be more prepared to listen (rather than merely hear the words) and to condition yourself to give attention more fully to the person to whom you are listening. Practising the 12 elements will improve all your relationships, and I encourage you to use these skills often.

Pick one element to focus on at a time, so you can more easily notice the difference, rather than trying to include them all at once and becoming overwhelmed. That way, you will appreciate the power and nuances of each of the elements.

In order to conceptualise these, they are divided into three distinct sections:

1. Preparing to listen (including rituals, a sense of curiosity and treating others as equals)

2. Distractions (how to be aware of and minimise them)

3. Enhancing Active Listening (using silence and being aware of the impact of body language).

Table 3.1: The 12 elements of Active Listening

The elements	What each element means
Preparing to listen	
1. Pre-listening agenda and questions: personal preparation	Awareness of your own rituals before you turn up to connect with others. This may include some mindful breathing or relaxation to become centred.
2. Judgement and equality	Suspending judgements and treating others as equals all contribute to being an active, empathic and deep listener.
3. Curiosity and interest	Cultivate a genuine desire to understand your client and their challenges. Be curious about what they may say next; don't second guess them. Think about how far they could go without your intervention.

Distractions	
4. Interrupting	Allow your desire to interrupt to pass without you speaking. Not being interrupted is so unusual that your client may be surprised at first, and then, when they realise you are not going to interrupt, you will notice them relaxing, not rushing their words and settling in to think more deeply.
5. Mobile phones	Research has shown that the mere presence of a mobile device and what it might represent (i.e. business connections, broader social network, etc.), can be distracting and have negative consequences in any social interaction. Ideally, put it away.
6. Multi-tasking or multi-focusing	We listen better and more actively when we focus on one activity at a time. The relevance here is to keep the focus on listening and staying curious about the speaker's message. Only consider what you will be saying when that time comes.
7. Avoid distracting the speaker	Keep a relaxed, neutral focus on the speaker as much as possible, and be mindful of the impact of your body language and non-verbal communication.

Enhancing Active Listening	
8. Breathing	If you take a deep breath in and out before speaking, for example when remaining silent, the speaker will, more often than not, speak some more.
9. Eye contact and body language	Be mindful that your eyes and your body convey your feelings, responses and thinking. It is also reassuring for the speaker, after they have looked away to think, to return and to see you are still looking at them.
10. Silence	Staying present and focused on the speaker means you have time to process and appreciate what they have to say. This contributes to creating safety and trust. This is a deliberate decision on the part of the listener to hold back from interrupting to the degree that supports the conversation.
11. Emotions and feelings	Be aware that being fully and unconditionally listened to may stir up unexpected emotions for the speaker. As the listener, treat all their reactions and responses as neutrally as possible. How you react or respond will be picked up by them, and therefore can make or break the conversation. The speaker will only open up emotionally to the depth at which they believe you can bear the weight of their story.

12. Opening question, and follow-on questions	How the listener opens the conversation is important. Open questions invite the speaker to decide what matters to them at that moment. When you think the speaker has finished, leave a longer pause and then ask, 'What more?,' as this can evoke further responses from them.

4. Connection

Connection is the culmination of all we have done before and has led us to this point. Connection is the threshold we need to cross as we move towards building even greater levels of rapport with the client. We are building a powerful, strong and engaged relationship. We will notice on many levels that something is starting to change between us and our client. There is likely to be a deeper sense of understanding or a feeling of ease and flow between us, or we seem to be in agreement with each other.

This is a critical point on the journey as it is proof that we have traversed the previous steps well and the client is right alongside us. We will know deep down if they are with us or not. If not, ask the client for honest, open feedback. If we are unable to reach Connection, we will fail, and neither of us will achieve our outcomes.

See Chapter 6: 'The Heart of the Matter: A New Interpretation of Emotions' by Dan Newby where he references emotions and listening beyond the words.

---

5. Empathy and building rapport

Empathy builds intimacy in relationships.

In this step, you start to really understand where the speaker is coming from as well as how they are feeling. Through being fully present, your mirror neurons enable you unconsciously to feel their feelings; you mirror their body language and positions and may even entrain with their breathing. The connection is deepening.

Research from Development Dimensions International (DDI) shows that leaders who master listening and respond with empathy will perform more than 40% higher in overall performance, coaching, engaging others, planning and organising, and decision-making.[3]

According to the *Oxford English Dictionary*, empathy is the 'ability to understand and share the feelings of another.' When a client says, 'Yes, you're right,' or 'You've got it!' you know that high level of rapport has been established. At this point, they may lean forwards and become more animated, as they wish to open up further, to share more, not just words, but feelings, and maybe explore 'that place' which is difficult for them to fully identify. Be comfortable to sit with them in this place.

6. Holding space and creating a safe place

Getting to this step takes time, as well as good, honest intention and patience. You will know when you have arrived at this place, as the relationship will feel different. Participants will be noticeably

---

3   'What's the number 1 leadership skill for overall success?,' *DDI*, 23 February 2016, https://www.ddiworld.com/global-offices/united-states/press-room/what-is-the-1-leadership-skill-for-overall-success

more relaxed with you. It is a place to honour. This will have been earned. It is freeing, liberating, inspiring and so much more.

When our environment feels safe, we are more likely to feel secure around others and know that they have our back, as we have theirs. We breathe more easily. We know that we can be open and honest, and know it will not lead to us being bullied, humiliated or rejected for what we say or do. We are increasingly likely to be more innovative, creative, challenging, resourceful, willing to be vulnerable, becoming more thoughtful, empathic and helpful. We will also offer more of our discretionary time for thinking and coming up with new ideas. It is the same for our clients.

Conversely, if the environment is unsafe, toxic or fearful, individuals become self-interested, self-serving, and unwilling to look out for or help others. They end up shutting down, keeping their heads below the parapet, whilst beginning to think, 'What's in it for me?,' and eventually becoming paranoid and stressed out. In the workplace, this can lead to higher rates of churn, absenteeism, presenteeism, and potentially long-term sickness or resignation.

In a two-year study, involving more than 180 teams, Google identified the underlying factors in their most effective project teams. They found that what really made a difference was the degree of psychological safety, i.e. an individual's perception of how emotionally safe it is to say or do something. This could be the difference between being in a team where there is no fear of the consequences of taking an interpersonal risk, and a team that interprets innovative individual behaviour or ideas as ignorant, incompetent, negative or disruptive.[4]

---

4   *re:Work*, https://rework.withgoogle.com/print/guides/5721312655835136/

7. Inspiring, influencing and achieving change

If the Relationship Journey has been travelled effectively, the client will be open and willing to suggest the way forward. They will be willing to climb the hill with us, brave the storm, and start moving together in the direction that best serves us all.

Appreciation and its impact on relationships

For any successful relationship, appreciation is needed. The Gottman Institute has identified what they call the 'magic relationship ratio,' [5] that is, the most effective ratio between appreciation and criticism being 5:1.

At the end of any conversation, take a moment to share what you appreciate about the speaker. There are many things to appreciate, such as their courage in sharing what they have shared, the commitment they are showing, their resilience, and so on. This further helps to engage the other person and make them feel valued. (This is not feedback, which is typically aimed at improving performance, but noticing and acknowledging their personal traits.)

---

5   'The magic relationship ratio, according to science,' *The Gottman Institute*, 4 October 2017, https://www.gottman.com/blog/the-magic-relationship-ratio-according-science/

CASE STUDY: ALWAYS ANOTHER WAY

My client, a successful CEO, was having challenges working with an operational team which was very remote from the main office. There were issues with some of the team, including the head of the team, around accountability, process improvement and internal and external communications.

From the outset, it was clear my client did not have colleagues with whom she felt safe enough to share her concerns or be able to think through possible solutions. In addition, I had a sense that she didn't need answers; rather, an opportunity to deeply explore the problems and solutions.

My approach was to create and hold a safe place for her to open up, and then to actively listen, remain curious, and seek to understand her and her situation.

Our first session was therefore relatively straightforward. I started the conversation with, 'Tell me about your remote operation?' At different times, perhaps when she stopped talking and was looking at me, I picked up on the last word or phrase that she had spoken and repeated it back to her, with a questioning tone or asking 'What more?' Most times though, my remaining silent and not interrupting was enough for her to continue talking.

Throughout the time I was with her, I demonstrated Active Listening: being fully present, eyes on hers, even when she was thinking and looking elsewhere, staying interested, sitting still with an open posture, remaining silent, nodding and offering facial expressions that showed I was fully with her.

It was noticeable as the sessions progressed how she started to relax more, opening up further and going deeper with her thinking. She found it easier and easier to just speak. She shared with me afterwards that it was rare to not be interrupted or to have advice thrust at her without it being requested.

Once we were able to 'get it all out,' it was much easier for her to highlight the different elements within the overall problem, and in doing so making it more manageable to address. It also made it easier for her to share the problems with others on her board and the remote team, such that she could solicit their thinking and possible solutions.

There was one moment, when she said, 'That's it, I have got it, thank you.'

The overall impact was that she could separate the big problem into a number of smaller elements and therefore find specific solutions. In addition, she had learned a valuable skill of listening for thinking, having experienced it fully herself.

A few months on, her remote operation was performing much better, in spite of the local environment. There have been some staff changes, and she has visited the remote team to engage more fully with them, though primarily to listen to them more actively first.

Coaching insights and summary

Active Listening is a core skill that enables you to build a deeper relationship with your client to facilitate behavioural change. It has 12 distinct elements, and, by practising them one at a time and integrating them into your practice, you will improve all of your relationships.

Developing a culture where Active Listening is the key foundation for 'the way we do things around here' positively increases the productivity of all our relationships and therefore the results we all produce.

In a highly competitive world where change is constant, our best strategy is to leverage the creativity and diversity of our employees and partner together effectively with our clients. Relationships are critical to business and personal success, and Active Listening is our key.

References

Bob Chapman and Raj Sisodia, *Everybody matters: the extraordinary power of caring for your people like family* (Penguin, 2016), see www.everybodymattersbook.com

Nancy Kline, *Time to think: listening to ignite the human mind* (Cassell Illustrated, 1999) and *More time to think: the power of independent thinking* (Fisher King, 2009), see www.timetothink.com

~

Connect with the Author

Thank you for reading this chapter. My intention is to provoke new thinking and inspire you to be more of an Active Listener so you transform your practice. For further details, to offer any feedback, to connect or to fully experience what it feels like to be heard, please get in contact with me: colin.smith@ dexteritysolutions.co.uk or www.dexteritysolutions.co.uk

II

THE UNCONSCIOUS MIND

Covered in this section

Whilst change begins at the conscious level, what we as coaches are seeking to achieve is to facilitate sustainable change that takes place at the unconscious level, where new behaviours occur automatically.

By unconscious, we mean everything that is outside a client's current conscious awareness; it is at this deeper level that we will be interacting so that we can facilitate and create lasting change more easily and effectively.

In the following two chapters, we are taken on a journey to discover how to use the powerful symbolism of the unconscious to influence transformation, as well as how to use key psychological principles to open clients' minds and gain new insights, and therefore the motivation and ability to change.

Chapter 4: Breaking Free: Unlocking Doors with Deep Reframing
Richard Haggerty

Richard shares with us Deep Reframing, a tool that helps locate new vantage points to reflect on problem situations, emotions or sense of identity, and fundamentally imbue them with new meaning. This in turn frees up mental, physical and emotional creative energy. Old problems therefore tend to appear less solid and more easy to overcome. In many cases, the problem as presented ceases to exist.

Chapter 5: Coaching the Unconscious Mind through Metaphor
Richard Haggerty

Richard takes us on a journey to generate deeper levels of being and awareness within a client and move them away from the 'old stories' that define and constrict their lives towards new ways of experiencing life and outcomes through the use of metaphors and stories. In this way, clients start to relate effortlessly and subconsciously to narratives that are empowering, create new perspectives, and enable them to move positively towards the outcomes they are seeking to achieve.

CHAPTER 4

BREAKING FREE

Unlocking Doors with Deep Reframing

Richard Haggerty

Human beings are meaning-making machines, yet that meaning is constructed mainly by default during our upbringing, including by family, friends, community and culture. This can create limits or blocks to what we think is possible. Deep Reframing changes this meaning and hence a person's perception of their ability to resourcefully handle problems and find creative solutions.

Covered in this chapter
- How to change beliefs using Deep Reframing
- Frames and how they determine our focus, meaning and reality
- The Reframing Mix: a novel way to develop unlimited reframes
- Outframing to channel energy and leverage motivation for change
- How to observe and test the effectiveness of reframes
- Case study of Deep Reframing from a client coaching session

---

INTRODUCTION

Imagine a new-born baby. From the moment they are born, they are told the meaning of each object and person, what is expected of them, what emotions are appropriate, and even what to believe is possible or 'realistic.' They are also told how to label objects and people by assigning them words and names, and very often, whether they are 'good' or 'bad.' A simple event occurs, for example it rains: 'Today is a miserable day' chimes the parent. Later, the child looks out of the window, grimaces and changes their mood to follow their parent's lead. They start interpreting the event in the same way automatically as though it is an objective fact.

Imagine further that this sequence of automatic labelling, dissecting and compartmentalising the world applies to all your thoughts – 'this is wrong,' 'this is difficult,' 'I can't do this' – and very soon you see how we are caught up in the matrix of our mind. We experience all of life (events, thoughts and feelings) through this lens. It becomes a room where we have unknowingly closed and bolted the doors. For simplicity, we will call these cognitive conclusions 'beliefs.'

Framing, therefore, is a natural process that results in us understanding the world in a highly individual way. Deep Reframing is a precise process to go deeply, beyond frames set by our default programming, to tap into the meaning-making machine inside a person. It has the potential to radically change a client's way of relating to the world and what they believe is possible. In contrast to standard reframing which presents a point of view, often consciously or by analogy, Deep Reframing seeks to change behaviours, outlook, and sense of efficacy to be able to deal with new situations. It does this by powerfully stacking a series of reframes to go more deeply into the unconscious and affect emotions, cognitions and identity. Deep Reframing helps the client to develop an expanded model of the world relative to their problem and outcomes.

Deep Reframing allows coaches to take an existing frame and ask, *If you experience it from this other perspective, how does that change things? What does it mean now?* Deep Reframing creates new vantage points from which to see our situation and allows us to change beliefs about what is and what is not possible. This, in turn, frees up mental and emotional creative energy, and creates a context in which transformation can occur.

Frames (of reference) have the power to support transformation because they allow coaches to communicate the message, *I want you to consider this situation, problem or relationship only in this way and in these terms*, but without actually saying those words. As coaches, we want to help the client to consider new perspectives, points of views, ideas, and possibilities. If we suggest that directly, we may run into resistance. In contrast, with Deep Reframing we imply there is new meaning, and create a context for a client to reflect in a way that leads to different perspectives, so they make new associations unconsciously.

Benefits of Deep Reframing in coaching

Deep Reframing offers these coaching advantages:

- Reframes are fast and straightforward ways to create change conversationally
- They empower clients to feel resourceful about dealing with challenges
- Beliefs that underpin problems change, disappear or lose their emotional intensity.

The systematic approach outlined in this chapter will help you:

- Understand the key variables in contexts that create meaning
- Learn how to establish frames and why frames control meaning
- Quickly eliminate competing beliefs that stop a client changing (outframing)
- Integrate a simple process to reframe any belief or problem
- Discover what to do after a reframe has been delivered to maximise its impact.

Context

All frames (of reference) exist within a context. Context can be thought of as the entirety of any situation and environment that creates the perception of meaning for an individual or group. It is impossible to think about framing or reframing without a basic understanding of context.

To clarify the concept of context, so it can be understood for coaches to work with it in a systematic way, I developed the Frames and Facts Context Model. In the diagram below, context is divided into two big picture parts, so you can see how fundamental it is to creating meaning:

- Frames
- Facts

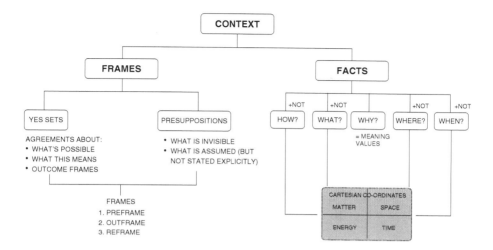

Figure 4.1: Frames and Facts Context Model

The division into 'facts' and 'frames' provides a systematic way for coaches to think about all the components of a specific context where a client is experiencing a problem or obstacle to achieving their outcome.

Chapter 2: 'Take the Plunge and Dive Deeper using Transactional Analysis' by Shirley Attenborough provides a clear and powerful systematic way to consider the structure of a client's problems, and select those aspects that may benefit from Deep Reframing.

Context component 1: Facts

Facts to investigate include:

- Who is there? Who is not present?
- What is going on? What is not happening that otherwise could be?
- Why is it happening? Why not?

- Where is it happening? Where is it not happening?
- When is it happening? When not?

If you employ this Context Model you have a powerful way to think about any situation more precisely. The 'facts of the matter' are what you might report to the police. These are the external objective facts that a person can observe and note.

Typically, we don't think about what is *not* happening, but this is often as important as what is happening. Think about some of the most significant moments in your life (weddings, holidays, successes, meeting friends, projects you have worked on). Imagine the most cheerful member of the group present. Now imagine they are gone, and the most obstructive person you can conceive of is there instead. You can already see that just one contextual variable makes all the difference. This is important because often what is not said or not considered will be exactly what the client needs to consider to be able to have a radical transformative shift in their thinking. Later on, we will consolidate and deepen this understanding of all the components of context that allow you to reframe (the 'Reframing Mix') so that you can play with these variables to generate unlimited scenarios and possibilities.

Context component 2: Frames

The second key component of context are frames (of reference). Frames of reference either create a context to allow certain ideas to be considered or close it down. For ease of understanding frames, I conceptualise them as consisting of:

- 'Yes' sets (agreements)
- Presuppositions (unspoken or tacit linguistic assumptions about reality)

1. 'Yes' sets are the individual agreements that you create with clients about:

    *   What is possible in a situation
    *   What it means
    *   Outcomes.

2. Presuppositions are hidden linguistic assumptions that presuppose things into existence. They might logically be true, given the parameters of what is said, but their foundational nature in propping up a problem may never have been fully noticed or questioned by the client. For example, if a client says, 'Another thing I need to be successful is a qualification,' this signals certain information, without saying so explicitly. You could logically infer:

    i.   the client doesn't think they are 'successful' now

    ii. they think they need a series of specific external achievements to be successful, which implies they don't think they can generate a sense of 'success' internally

    iii. they use the word 'need' which implies they feel they *must* have this, rather than coming from choice

    iv. a corollary of this is that they may not feel very positive or calm, but they *have* to struggle to achieve objectives in order to feel better about their current situation and relieve the pressure of what they perceive they 'need' to make them 'successful.'

At this point, even with just one sentence, a coach has a lot of options about what aspect of the presuppositions underpinning the problem they want to challenge or question: a goldmine for Deep Reframing.

Framing in stages

To create a context in which new ideas or possibilities are accepted by the client, we may have to present a number of frames or reframes that allow for that. For example, *You can restructure your business* may be too much too soon. A frame of, *Let's examine ways in which businesses can adapt to change* could open that door. The key is to become aware of the possibilities that a client will entertain, and then gradually reframe those possibilities they won't – to the degree that is helpful and aligned with their coaching outcomes. In this way, frames are master suggestions because they imply that the client can perceive and interact with the world in a particular way: for example, full of potential and options, or laden with rigid procedures or personal history that seemingly can't be changed.

Below I outline a unique method in which you can apply any reframing patterns you might choose to use. As long as you understand that reframes only exist in context, that you may need to plan a sequence of frames that your client may benefit from – and only proceed once you have agreement – you are ready to experience the magic of reframing.

THE REFRAMING MIX

The Reframing Mix has 6 steps. Following these will move your client through the reframing process quickly and effectively. The 6 steps are:

1. Identify problem and outcomes
2. Outframe all other beliefs and problems
3. Deliver reframe using the Reframing Mix
4. Follow-up questions and testing
5. Cycle through steps 3–4 until shift occurs
6. Notice new choices and future pace.

A more in-depth explanation of Active Listening and its role in coaching can be found in Chapter 3: 'The Transformational Impact of Active Listening' by Colin D. Smith. A key strategy to maintain rapport (so clients accept reframes) is through effective listening accompanied by a curious and compassionate non-judgemental attitude.

1. Identify problem and outcomes

When we set frames, we say what the purpose or wider meaning of something is. The frame is where we specify the lens through which we will be examining a situation. This could be as simple as telling a story or metaphor to establish a frame that 'change is possible' or 'people can go through difficult changes and transform and grow.'

Remember, the frame controls the meaning, so you can be as overt as you need to be here. You might say, *Today we are going to look at this one problem and help you explore some ways of looking at it that can help allow creative solutions to start appearing spontaneously or at least give enough distance from that situation to begin assessing new options. Would that be OK with you?*

Identify specific problem or belief
Clarity is key to Deep Reframing. The belief or problem needs to be small enough to tackle. 'My life is a wreck' can be reframed, but it is easier to work with 'I have a work presentation coming up in three weeks in front of 100 people, I am nervous, and want to feel x, y and z.'

To assist with reframing it helps to know:

- A specific situation, scenario or event (past or present)
- One or more triggers (what they see or hear that is keeping the problem active)
- How it makes the client feel
- How they want to feel differently
- What it means to the client.

Again, you can frame this as part of the process to reassure your client that this indeed can benefit other areas of their life.

A coach can outframe successfully by, for example, explaining to the client that they will deal with one aspect of the problem at a time: each shift in perspective helps build critical mass to support their overall outcome.

2. Outframe all other beliefs and problems

Once you have a specific belief or problem, it is relatively easy to outframe other considerations. Outframing is a way of communicating that all other problems can be parked for a while. This helps both coach and client focus on one issue at a time.

So, if the client says, 'I would like to do that, but I don't have enough time,' you can outframe: *It seems like you have some concerns about time management. We can certainly address those in a later session.*

Note that the problem above of 'I don't have enough time' is really a belief (perception) accompanied by a strong emotion. It is important to help the client see that the problem, as presented, ultimately consists of a series of beliefs because you can then deal with them one at a time. This helps overcome the client's emotion and limited thinking to develop practical steps to achieve their desired outcome. In this case, you can return to the sense of 'I don't have enough time' after reframing the first problem. This only becomes problematic if you don't outframe (i.e. hold off dealing with them until later) all the residual beliefs that unpin the problem because it then becomes a hydra with too many heads to tackle at one time.

Outframing is an essential step because it gives the coach a way to communicate, *Out of all the ways of looking at the world, you are only going to look at this one belief or scenario now, which means you can channel all your available energy into this one problem in light of everything else in your life, every learning, insight and resource you have ever tapped into and more.* In other words, clients will be focusing all their available energy on solving one aspect of a problem rather than shifting focus or avoiding the issue because it is uncomfortable.

3. Deliver reframe using the Reframing Mix

REFRAMING MIX

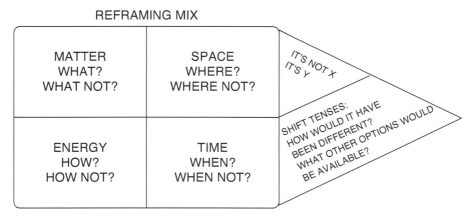

X = PROBLEMS AS PRESENTED / PERCEIVED

Y = OTHER WAYS OF PERCEIVING
SITUATION USING THE REFRAMING MIX

Figure 4.2: Reframing Mix

The Reframing Mix is a beautiful and simple way to generate reframes: using the four spacetime dimensions of space, time, energy, matter (the scientific explanation of the fabric of reality), this is a systematic way to create unlimited new perspectives for clients to consider.

This also helps coaches to get away from using dead reframes i.e. pre-packaged reframes that have been used so many times that they have lost their power: for example, 'This isn't a problem. It's a challenge.'

The Reframing Mix divides up reality into four quadrants (also called 'Cartesian Co-ordinates') of spacetime:

- Space
- Time
- Energy
- Matter.

It says, if you are thinking about reframing, then pick any one or more of these elements that create the (perceived reality of a) context and see what happens when they are included or excluded.

Let's say we pick matter and time. A client has a presenting problem of 'motivation to complete a major project at work.' It gives a coach countless ways to approach this:

- *If you had an extra person helping you for part of that time, how would that feel different?*
- *If you had half the time, but twice the energy, how much more compelling would that be?*
- *If you didn't have that deadline, but had more space available to do it, what would be different?*

We are not necessarily looking for a logical solution to emerge from the reframe; rather we are at this point helping dissolve the mental cement that has held the problem in place.

Redefining the problem or belief
We can go further and use the Reframing Mix for a specific type of reframe called a 'redefine.' This simple pattern starts with:

'**it's not that**…' and ends with '**it's that**…' [and add a follow-up question to cement change].

In other words:

- A does not equal B (A ≠ B)
- A equals C (A = C)
- + follow-up question

Deep Reframing examples: using time
It's not that you're not motivated, it's that the timeframe is too long / too short. How would it be different if you had twice the time / an enforced deadline?

It's not that there isn't time, it's the timing. If you had this to do last year before this current situation, how would that have felt different? As you consider that and look to the future, what else feels different?

Deep Reframing examples: using energy and space
It's not that you aren't motivated because you have a lot of energy around this; it's just that you need space to reflect and tap into the full range of emotions you possess. If you had absolute clarity about how to proceed, how much more energy would you have now that you're motivated?

It's not that the problem is motivation; it's that you are too motivated to get it right. If you had more distance to consider this problem – like you were thinking about one of your international teams that was trying to figure this exact problem out somewhere else thousands of miles away – how would that be different? How would your perspective already have changed?

The beauty of the Reframing Mix is that you can challenge any aspect of what the client believes is reality to help shift their perspective.

My coach once asked me, 'How close are you to your big vision?' I hesitated and replied, 'I think I can achieve this goal in three years, but definitely in five.' I started to feel under pressure as it was a HUGE goal. Martijn looked at me and followed up, 'How would you feel about that vision if time didn't exist?' That one question caused me to stop, and totally consider my vision outside the frame of reference I had unconsciously linked to it: the perceived pressure of time. It instantly reframed my experience.

You are communicating covertly as a subtext in all the questions: *Given the inclusion or absence of this aspect of time, energy, space, and matter, how does that change your perspective, meaning, and relationship to that old problem?*

4. Follow-up questions and testing

Follow-up question or suggestion to cement change
Offering a reframe is potentially helpful, but it's like saying, 'Hey, if you take the wall down in your lounge, look how it opens things out.'

People tend to try to brick that back up because they feel comfortable with what is. So when you start to get a shift, you want to cement in the new perspective or belief quickly by immediately following up with a question or suggestion.

The first reframe may have opened a door, but it is immediately after that when mental and emotional energy is high and often still in a state of chaos (a state of possibility): it's an ideal time for the client to walk through the door and experience the new frame of reference more fully, before that energy dissipates.

Merely giving some general suggestions can be enough to help the client consider the reframe more fully:

- *Think about that*
- *Consider that for a while*
- *Does that make sense now?*
- *How do you feel about that old problem now?*

Sit back, listen and be patient as you ask your client to reflect on their experience.

Observe reaction
New coaches want to know, *How will I know my reframe worked? How do I know my coaching has been successful?*

The answer: your client will confirm it for you if you are attentive.

After each suggestion and reframe, notice what happens. The simplest way to think about this is, 'Does my client look happier now or less resourceful?' Remember you can always ask a client, so you never need to guess the impact of it. Ask, *So how are you feeling now? What shifted for you? What feels different?*

Test
Ask your client, *As you think about that old problem, how do you feel different now?*

Again, observe their response because they will often say, 'I feel better BUT…'

That 'but' is an indication to take whatever they present and use as the next reframe.

5. Cycle through steps 3–4 until shift occurs

Repeat steps 3–4 with whatever is left of the problem or belief. Just pick the next reframe that looks promising – whatever hasn't been resolved from step 4. Take your time, maintain rapport, slow down if necessary. There is no rush. If they only get a small shift, that is great feedback for the next cycle.

Stay curious, fascinated and keep your focus on your client.

6. Notice new choices and future pace

Once your reframes seem to have created a shift, then introduce more powerful tests to see how solid the change is. If a transformation has occurred, a client will naturally tend to have a more powerful belief that they can now do what they felt they could not do before.

If a client says they are over their phobia of presenting, then say, *Wonderful, how would you feel about presenting to 20 of my clients who are coming in this afternoon?* Stop and watch their reaction as you simulate them feeling caught out in life. What happens? The best place to test your work is inside your coaching session and by picking progressively more challenging scenarios. That way, you can reframe anything left of the old problem that the client was not previously aware of, in the time you have available.

Notice new choices

Pay attention to what your client is experiencing that is different.

Ask them questions about it:

- *How do things feel different now?*
- *Wow, that seems like a big shift. Tell me a bit more about that? What's going on for you?*

You want to notice especially:

- Changes in physiology (body posture, facial expressions, smiles, bright eyes, etc.)
- How much more energy they have
- Levels of enthusiasm.

You compare these to how they were when they first started talking about their challenge.

Agree next action and future pace

Effective coaching ultimately requires an agreement and commitment to take defined action. The energy released by reframing can initially be fragile, so it is important to consolidate the shift as much as possible by creating momentum through action.

When a client takes action, they have an internal need to be consistent with that behaviour, or they risk experiencing cognitive dissonance as they practise new identity forms. As coaching sessions progress and the new way of being becomes entrenched, you are then able to get progressively bigger agreements.

CASE STUDY: DEEP REFRAMING TO ADOPT THEIR NEW POINT OF VIEW

Deep Reframing allows you to get very creative: for example, using 'imagination experiments' with the Reframing Mix. In the following case study, my client's emotion was so intense that he was shaking with anger / rage even though it had been twenty years since the incident. It was clear to me that he perceived a great injustice had been done. The real impact though was the way it was now affecting his current relationships.

Steps 1–2: Identify problem and outcomes / outframe
The client had a pressing concern with the way he was 'reacting with anger in work situations and couldn't figure out why.' He knew he didn't want to behave in this way and told me it felt disproportionate to the perceived trigger, but he had no idea consciously how to change. He wanted instead to be able to handle any difficult conversations or ambiguous communication to be more influential and maintain effective working relationships.

My client shared that during a recent snowfall a colleague suggested that people in some areas would find it easier than others to get to work. My client had taken this as a personal slight because he lived in one of the alleged 'easy to get to work' areas, and he knew that snowfall was very high and had made the roads impassable. He had even injured himself trying to get into work in deep snow and had to return home.

I gently asked, *That feeling you felt when your colleague spoke to you, where did it come from?* He immediately remembered an experience of being in the college canteen when he was younger.

I asked him, *So what happened in the canteen?* And he replied, 'I was sitting there with my friends kicking back, and there was also a girl I didn't know.'

At one point one of his classmates said something, and he started laughing out loud.

He couldn't even remember what they were laughing about. All he could remember was that suddenly, for no obvious reason, the girl turned to him and screamed, 'Why are you laughing? You're ugly.'

As he relayed this all those years later, he was clearly still infuriated. I asked, *Do you think that somebody who is asking those sorts of questions or who's saying 'you are ugly' is happy inside themselves?*

He replied, 'No.'

Step 3: Deliver reframe using Reframing Mix – 'It's not that…it's that' + follow-up questions
I continued, *Well think about this for a minute. It's not that it was anything personal. It's that this person (and we don't know anything about her life) may have had the most horrible time at home and school and had been teased. It's that she may have been humiliated and bullied and whenever people do that, whenever kids or family members do that and laugh, it can make a person feel incredibly embarrassed and self-conscious. Does that make sense?*

I said, *We're only guessing here, but imagine if it's that she had been bullied so much and every time people were laughing at her – and this has been going on for years and years – she felt powerless to do anything about it. Now all of a sudden here she is in the canteen and somebody starts to laugh loudly and abruptly.*

[Since the reframe was having an impact, I was able to deliver these follow-up questions. The key was to pause after asking each one – to allow him time to process the idea I was presenting.]

How is she likely to feel?

What if it's that the sound of laughter is so strongly associated with humiliation that she feels that way immediately?

What if it's that it triggers that feeling in her automatically and she had no way to deal with it because instantly inside her mind there was this torrent of abuse and this horrible feeling welling up inside her.

What do kids do when somebody insults them?

[At this point, I paused and made sure my client had processed this question because it opened the way for Deep Reframing using empathy and identity.]

When a kid is insulted if somebody says 'You're fat,' they immediately turn that round on them and say 'No, you're fat.'

So if people had been calling her ugly and laughing at her and completely inadvertently her feelings had been triggered inside her, isn't it fair to say that it's nothing about you: it's everything about her and about the difficulties and issues she's experienced?

And what if this experience was so traumatic for her that the only way she would be able to even protect herself was to say that very phrase?

Wouldn't that mean that she was trying to protect herself and that it was nothing about you?

Step 4: Follow-up questions and testing
As you think about it from this perspective, how do you feel different?'

My client looked at me, and he said, 'You know, I think that I feel a bit sorry for her' and then came the kicker. He said, 'You know, the thing that hurt at the time was that I believed what she was saying that I'm not that good-looking and it really struck a nerve with me.'

I looked at my client and asked, *So how do you feel about that now?*

He replied, 'I feel at peace inside myself and I understand that nothing that was coming from that person was anything to do with me. It was all about her life. I'll never know exactly what was going on inside, or the cause of that, but I do know that it wasn't from a place of happiness and peace and I know it was nothing about me.'

Step 5: Cycle through steps 3–4 until shift occurs
In this case, we moved on to noticing new choices and future pacing. You may find that clients need to repeat steps 3–4 and reframe other aspects of the problem, until they experience a visible emotional shift.

Step 6: Notice new choices and future pace
At this point I asked my client to consider how he felt about the situation at work, so he could join up the dots and make the association between the initial sensitising event and his present-day interactions. He appreciated that the old conditioning had played a part and that he now felt fine about it. I asked him to consider how he would behave and feel differently with this shift, and if someone mentioned

something factually incorrect about him in the future. He said he would monitor his reactions with senior colleagues over the next week and report back what he noticed that was different in his interactions.

Deep Reframing allows the coach to create and test scenarios that give birth to new frames of reference, and tap into vast reservoirs of creative potential. Constructing a plausible narrative allowed my client time to explore a new universe of possibility and meaning.

My client in this case study experienced a shift, even though this was a simple imagination experiment. We had no information about the girl who had made the comment in the canteen. But shifting the frame from 'I was deliberately wronged' to 'she was suffering and completely unconscious in her reaction, which I inadvertently triggered,' allowed for a transformation.

Constructing a plausible narrative allowed my client time to explore a new universe of possibility and meaning. I nudged and guided, but allowed him to have his experience and reach his own conclusions.

Notice how I included elements of the Reframing Mix throughout including location (space), what came before (time), people (matter) and emotions (energy) here to set up a number of new ways of experiencing the original problem differently.

Using Deep Reframing in coaching creates opportunities for changing a sense of identity. For more information on elegantly coaching at the level of identity, please read Chapter 10: 'Coaching for Identity Grows Purpose and Performance' by Aidan Tod.

Coaching insights and summary

Deep Reframing enables a coach to change the meaning of a client's experience and hence their personal reality. Typical implications (beliefs) hidden inside problems that clients bring to coaching sessions include:

- I can't do this
- I am not worthy
- It is too difficult
- I just can't see a solution.

When you help your client to reframe their beliefs, you are giving them a ring of keys and asking them to try out different doors to see what happens. Just the process of exploring together using the Reframing Mix in a safe and non-judgemental context will tend to dissolve the mental cement of the old problem.

By using the Reframing Mix, maintaining rapport through creating an ongoing sense of safety, and a heightened awareness of context, all your coaching sessions will become enriched and more satisfying. In the next chapter, we will look at a precise way of reframing and influencing change: the power of metaphor.

Coaching in action

Theory

All problems and solutions are dependent on meaning. Ascribe new meaning at the deepest level, and a profound sense of freedom emerges.

Action

Begin playing with the Reframing Mix. Over the next few days, when clients or friends start telling you their problems, listen carefully and with compassion.

Gently start asking questions about who was there / not there (matter), when it happened (time), where it occurred (space) and how it transpired (energy).

Now ask clients and friends how it would be different if one variable changed, e.g. the location, someone being there or not there, the energy or intensity of the situation and when – whether it was in the past, present or future.

If they are unsure how to reply, ask again or choose another variable. Keep things light throughout and make sure to maintain rapport.

Pay special attention to when they really have to think about the question and its implications. Give them time to consider your question and notice how it starts to shift their emotional reaction and associated cognitions.

~

Connect with the Author
Thank you for taking the time to read this chapter. If you are feeling excited about the possibilities of using reframing for coaching and in your day-to-day life, I congratulate you! As you start using Deep Reframing, you may consider how use of the techniques, tools, and strategies in this chapter can be applied more widely in your business or personal life. Contact me to fully explore further creative methods for generating lasting change at: richard@richardhaggerty.co.uk or visit www. RichardHaggerty.co.uk

CHAPTER 5

COACHING THE UNCONSCIOUS MIND THROUGH METAPHOR

Richard Haggerty

Metaphors contain powerful symbols and emotions, and offer unique approaches for coaches to keep sessions creative, stimulating and transformative. By understanding how to use symbols and emotions in coaching, coaches can support clients to discover new abilities and resources that help them make changes – spontaneously – with little or no conscious interference from the analytical mind.

Covered in this chapter

- Key psychological principles that explain how metaphors create change
- Introducing metaphors naturally into a coaching session
- Developing transformational coaching metaphors using a coach's personal life experiences
- The mental process a coach needs to adapt metaphors for a client
- Identifying symbols that provide the fuel for metaphors to be transformative
- Case studies using metaphors from real-world coaching sessions

---

INTRODUCTION

Working at the level of metaphor is like discovering a fragrant new spice to add to a dish and makes coaching more satisfying and richer. Like any spice, you won't need to use it all the time, and sometimes less is more.

What is a metaphor? In this context, it is when one thing (an idea, feeling, word, image, place, person, symbol, etc.) represents something else. In practice, metaphors in coaching tend to be either short sayings (e.g. epithets) or stories of varying lengths. These are not literary stories so much as a coach's own, or other people's, meaningful life experiences that they adapt and bring to bear to support a client in achieving their outcomes. The power comes from a conversation where a client's conscious mind is focused on one meaning, but their unconscious mind (the storehouse of habits, emotions and potential) is being stimulated to develop other resourceful meanings, options, and emotions that make it possible for new behaviours to manifest.

Benefits of metaphor in coaching

Working at the level of metaphor gives a coach unique advantages in conducting sessions:

- Stay fresh and maintain the client's interest in the coaching process
- Trigger specific emotions by telling a story that maps on to those emotions
- Assist the client's creative inner mind in generating solutions spontaneously
- Set strong frames for a session (called a pre-frame)
- Present new perspectives to the unconscious mind with no resistance (called a reframe).

The systematic approach outlined in this chapter will help you:

- Gain confidence by developing metaphors from your own life experience
- Use successes with previous clients as metaphors you tell new clients
- Deliver transformative stories that open a client's mind to possibilities
- Keep a client connected to positive inner resources
- Minimise potential objections a client has to making changes
- Introduce metaphors in a way that is consistent with wider coaching objectives.

Priming and the law of association

We leverage two psychological principles in our understanding of the power of metaphor to create change.

Firstly, basic learning and neurology are strongly influenced by the contiguity *law of association.* According to Wikipedia: 'In cognitive science, association by contiguity is the principle that ideas, memories, and experiences are linked when one is frequently experienced with the other.'[1] In other words, we fundamentally learn by pairing things, often by linking new information to something existing.[2] This is most useful when the automatic association and pairing cause us to feel more resourceful and have a strong sense of self-efficacy.

---

1   'Contiguity (psychology),' *Wikipedia*, https://en.wikipedia.org/w/index. php?title=Contiguity_(psychology)&oldid=863861289
2   N.E. Spear, B.R. Ekstrand and B.J. Underwood 'Association by contiguity' in *Journal of Experimental Psychology*, 67 (2), 151–161, 1964.

Secondly, metaphor taps into the power of *priming*. According to Wikipedia, 'Priming is a technique whereby exposure to one stimulus influences a response to a subsequent stimulus, without conscious guidance or intention.'[3] Psychological research on priming suggests that symbols such as auditory and visual primes (words, sounds, images or pictures) can have rapid and measurable effects on behaviour when they are appropriate to the person, culture, and context. Furthermore, Doyen et al. (2012) have highlighted that 'both priming and experimenters' expectations are instrumental in explaining the [...] effect.'[4] In other words, the key to successful use of priming is to ensure that the experimenter (coach) has total belief and positive expectation of what the effect will be. In this chapter, you will discover how to deepen that expectation inside the mind of a coach through imbuing symbols with the coach's own cognitive and emotional associations within metaphors. By doing so, a deeper level of positive anticipation is already activated and present, which ultimately makes metaphors impactful for the client.

Using these two principles, priming and the law of association, coaching metaphors help clients transform by influencing their emotions and attitudes, and therefore behaviours.

---

3   'Priming (psychology), *Wikipedia*, https://en.wikipedia.org/wiki/index.%20 php?title=Priming_(psychology)&oldid=877889823

4   Stéphane Doyen, Olivier Klein, Cora-Lise Pichon and Axel Cleeremans (2012) 'Behavioral priming: It's all in the mind, but whose mind?,' *PloS one*. 7. e29081, p.1. 10.1371/journal.pone.0029081

The 7 steps to creating effective coaching metaphors

A simple structure to deliver coaching metaphors is:

1. **Identify the client's problem and outcomes**. When eliciting these, make a mental or written note of three to five specific words or phrases that clients use, so, when you tell a metaphor, you mirror these: include problem 'hot words' at the beginning of the story and outcome phrases or descriptions at the end, so their unconscious mind can firmly establish the connection between the story and the client's situation more easily. Hot words include values which are key drivers of motivation in our lives. These words are powerful because they are automatically associated with deep emotions.

To learn more about how to elicit and work with values conversationally so you can include them when coaching the unconscious mind through metaphor, please see Chapter 9: 'Values: Developing a Powerful Guidance System' by David Ross.

---

2. **Pick a simple story that has great significance and meaning in your life**. There need be no obvious conscious link to the client's problem or context and the metaphor you tell. Consider how elements of that story could become symbols that relate to your client's journey (see 'Metaphor coaching in action' below for a full process).

3. **Make sure the client is fully associated with their outcome** by repeating it back to them: they should be fully considering it, and excited or inspired in some

way. Associated here means a client will feel as if they have already achieved their outcome. As much of their awareness as possible must be thinking about what they want and imagining what it will do for them. This primes them fully to make unconscious connections from the story that will follow, even though they are never instructed to make that connection consciously.

4. **Casually tell the story** once you establish rapport. Pause periodically to allow time for the client to process, bathe in the positive feelings and explore their internal world long enough to appreciate that something significant is happening.

5. **Incorporate subtle changes in physiology or body language** that you observe clients manifesting into the story. If they start to relax while telling the story, mention how a character in the story begins to relax.

6. **End story and change topic**. Let the metaphor do its job. Never explain a metaphor.

7. **Follow up and ratify changes**. In the next session, find out how they have been impacted without mentioning the story specifically. Ask, *How are you doing? What's changed?*

Bringing your client into the story

Metaphors can be used to prepare your client's mind for success once you have established enough rapport and created a strong sense of anticipation. One story can be adapted to almost any problem or performance objective when told in the right context and at the appropriate time.

I use 'The Golden Ring' story below with clients for a range of problems and performance outcomes. A client had a difficulty discovering their over-arching business vision and committing to something worthwhile. After we had elicited the problem (stuck and drifting), identified the outcome (clear focus), I reflected on how certain symbols in the story related to his situation. I then told the metaphor.

It is important to observe your client keenly as you tell the story, so you can make it more immediately relevant to them. As before, if you see them take a deep breath, then shortly afterward in your story, you might say *...and they took a deep breath and relaxed.* That way, their unconscious mind will 'get' that this story is intended for them, but without having to say it explicitly, which could trigger a cycle of conscious interference or performance anxiety.

Remember, the law of association means their unconscious mind is always linking ideas together. If the unconscious mind hears, 'They took a deep breath and relaxed,' then the listener's unconscious mind joins up the dots and makes the associational link, 'Hey, I just did that: I breathed, therefore I must be relaxing.' Taking something that is happening in the environment and giving it immediate meaning and relevance by pairing it with something non-related is called utilisation, and is a powerful way to link suggestions you give to the client.

Metaphor: The Golden Ring

When I was nine years old, I went fishing in the Indian Ocean with my dad, one of his Sudanese friends, and a local Tanzanian fisherman called Captain Saidi.

We lived in Dar es Salaam at that time, and this was the most exciting adventure I could imagine. I got to spend time with my dad, be with the grown-ups, and go out in one of the fishing boats I always saw local fishermen use. We had little wooden hand lines to fish with, which were bits of driftwood with fishing wire wrapped around them, a hook on the end, and a whole bunch of squid that would lure fish. There was also one essential tool: a sharp knife to chop the bait.

We set off from the beach into the beautiful Tanzanian sea, deep into the Indian Ocean. Captain Saidi was long-sighted, so he could see in the distance where the seagulls were gathering over the sea. Throughout the day, he would use the gathering of birds as a signal to guide us to where fish were abundant; he would then pull the chord for the engine and take us in his little wooden boat, powered by an equally tiny motor, in that direction. And we knew, once we got there, that it was going to be a bountiful time because Barnabas, my dad's friend, put a bit of squid on the handline, dropped it over the side, tugged, pulled it back and, at once, there on the end was a large beautiful red snapper fish. And the pile of fish just seemed to keep growing and growing in the boat all day as we caught more and more. We returned a lot of fish to the sea because they were too small to eat.

All of a sudden, Barnabas turned to me and said, 'Richard, my wedding ring has dropped off my finger to the bottom of the ocean, and I need you to go and get it back.'

Now it's really interesting because I had no fear of water and I was a confident swimmer, but you have to realise that we were in the middle of the Indian Ocean. You couldn't see land in any direction you looked. But my dad was there, and I didn't want to let him down. I wanted him to be proud of me.

I asked Barnabas what colour his ring was and he explained that it was gold.

So, I got into the water, and you know obviously the first thing is to make sure no large fins are sticking out of the water because there were barracuda in the vicinity and it just seemed like a good thing to check for. The next thing is I needed to check the depth. I knew I was very good at holding my breath but I wanted to know two things: exactly where the location was of the ring that I was going to get back, and how quickly and deeply I was going to have to dive down, so that I could psychologically prepare myself to get down there and make sure that I had enough oxygen to get back up to the surface safely.

And so the first time, I dived down to get a sense of where the ring was. I held my breath and went under, and I realised it was indeed quite deep. It was doable. It was deeper than I'd ever been before, quite a bit deeper, and I realised that my nemesis [as far as I was concerned when I was nine years old] was on the bottom: a whole family of giant sea urchins. Their black, moving, twisting, foot-long spindly sharp poisoned barbs were looking at me and glimmering. Right in the middle of where they were, I could see Barnabas's ring.

The second time I dived, I needed to get a real sense of the depth and a more precise location of the ring. I was able to descend a bit deeper and see exactly where it was, where I needed to get to and where I was going to reach and place my hand to pick up this golden treasure on the bed of the sea. Then I came up again for air.

As I was treading water and breathing after surfacing, I played the scenario in my mind of how deep I was going to go, the specific direction I was going to head in, how I was going to grab the ring, what it would feel like to hold it and what it was going to take for me to get back up again. I took three slow, deliberate deep breaths and went for it.

I pushed myself down as quickly as I could go with all my strength and energy, slowing down just above the sea urchins, knowing that they were a few inches below me and yet just next to them somehow missing the whole bed of them was the ring. I carefully leaned over, picked it up and started on my journey up, and I knew that there was going to be the hardest part yet. So I concentrated on feeling my body comfortably and quickly moving up at a consistent speed yet still conserving enough energy to keep moving. Quicker and quicker, I started to go up. And I could see the light above me and knew exactly where I was heading and that I was going to get there. I kept going and going and going with the ring in hand, telling myself, 'Nearly there. You can do this. You can do this. You will do this,' and I kept pushing and pushing. Even though I felt my lungs bursting for oxygen, I kept pushing and pushing upwards until I could see the light of the midday sun streaming through the water.

All of a sudden, my head exploded through the surface of the water. Oxygen flooded inside my lungs and I breathed gratefully. I looked around for the boat, swam over to it and smiled as I handed Barnabas his wedding ring.

Metaphor coaching in action

Let us consider how the elements of the story could relate to your client's journey. You may be wondering what connections I saw between the diving story and my client being 'stuck and drifting' and seeking 'clear focus.' The steps below explain how to modify and adapt a story to create an unconscious relationship with the client's situation. Certain elements naturally get emphasised or deprioritised after going through this process.

Symbols of power

Establish the meaning you would like to sub-communicate by reflecting on your own experiences in light of the problem and specific outcomes that your client has. There are 4 steps to achieve this:

Step 1: Choose symbols

The first step is to pick 'symbols' from the story. Between three and seven symbols is ample. Symbols include visuals, sounds, concepts, ideas or feelings that stand out to you. Go with the first images, ideas or sensations that come to mind – without censoring. There is no right or wrong. These are simply elements that jump out for you. This is important because the first step to developing a compelling metaphor is the coach trusting their unconscious mind and associations to a story. By trusting the symbols, you already start to make the story 'yours.'

One possible list (of many):

- Boat
- Captain
- Fishing line
- Birds
- Fish
- Sun
- Diving down.

Step 2: Link symbols to an outcome

Ask yourself *What could these symbols represent in relation to the client's outcome?*. The entire process could be done in five minutes or less once you become familiar with it. In this case, the outcome is moving from stuck to having a clear focus. Go with your gut instincts and note whatever comes to mind:

- The boat could represent having a solid base. It's like having certainty in your abilities.
- The captain makes me think of the conscious mind. He / she is in charge but needs the crew to support them to move in a certain direction. But the captain is totally responsible for conveying that message.
- Fishing line makes me think of searching for clarity. It's like looking for something certain to hold on to. If the first place you go to has no fish, then move somewhere else. Be patient. Sit with it.
- Birds make me think about that wider perspective looking down on life and seeing what matters. It's not the money … not even recognition. Rather it is your relationships and health. Fulfilment. Soaring above to look down at everyone below makes me think about what truly matters.
- Fish make me think about the absolute abundance of food for thought and ideas that is there beneath the sea (subconscious mind).
- Diving down makes me think about how I will know I have found something valuable. I have to wait until there is something that I can notice that is going to add tangible value, feels good, is absolutely the right thing and then not just stick a toe in the water, go right in. You can only go down a few metres at first and may feel out of your depth. But then you soon grow in confidence. Once you know what you want, you get going.

- As a Gestalt, the golden ring metaphor could relate to starting out feeling stuck and yet having the support of the captain and shipmates you trust (a coach) and being willing to trust the sea (your inner potential).

Step 3: Tell the metaphor

Remember, the meaning of symbols is for the coach only, so that they will sub-communicate key messages in the story through tonality changes, shifts in emotion and subtle changes in their physiology and body language. At this point, the coach has a deep unconscious relationship to symbols, which in turn achieves two outcomes for priming:

i. it naturally amplifies their own positive expectation of its potential positive effects as they tell it because the coach is now primed to tell the story with a strong sense of anticipation

ii. they will be priming the client's unconscious mind using both symbols that link to their problem as well as specific problem and outcome words and phrases that were elicited from the client at the beginning of the session.

To deliver a metaphor effectively:

- Develop a 'storyteller voice,' laden with implication. Some coaches like to think back to being told stories as a child if that ignites their imagination. Others might enjoy listening to audio books for inspiration. Above all, think about the way you would talk to a dear friend when telling them about a significant experience (e.g. something that happened on holiday)
- A storyteller uses emphasis by changing their tone of voice on certain phrases and words and using gestures as appropriate

- A storytelling voice naturally becomes more engaging and charismatic when varying the speed of speaking and punctuating with pauses
- Trust and 'know' that this is how your unconscious mind is communicating with theirs. The work in connecting the left brain (analytical) with the right brain (emotional subconscious) has already been done quietly inside the coach's mind. Of course, left and right brain are metaphors too!

Step 4: Finish and change topic

Clients are fascinated when coaches tell stories because they keep the coaching experience novel, fresh and engaging. At the end of the story, resist the temptation to succumb to that fascination and explain the meaning, thereby making it into a conscious analogy. Instead, as you finish, change the topic of conversation and carry on with the session. Like a seed you have planted, allow the metaphor time to germinate and take root. Metaphors work outside the conscious mind and keep coaching sessions engaging. They help clients make their meaning and develop new solutions and perspectives in their own time.

Introducing coaching metaphors

As long as you have enough rapport, a client will be willing to listen and ascribe meaning and significance to whatever you do or say. At a natural point in a coaching session where rapport and trust are established, and the coach has the client's attention, they can begin to tell metaphors.

For effect, it is often worth pausing, taking a deep breath and looking meaningfully at your client for a few moments to let them know that what follows is going to be important. Everything you are doing implies that this has significant meaning.

Consider this simple way to introduce a story naturally to a coaching session:

A client I knew had a similar experience to you. And it made me think of this story… Several years ago, a son went fishing with his father and a wise old local fisherman… a very special moment…

Or you could say, *This reminds me of a story that I once read…*

Developing metaphors

You have a wealth of stories from your own life experience. So what makes a metaphor worth honing and developing to use with clients?

There are five criteria for selecting powerful and effective metaphors for change:

1. **Pick an event or activity that has significant meaning (emotion) for you**. You should be actively doing something in this story, not passive. Pick something where you are physically using your body so that this is an active metaphor because, after all, in coaching we want to move clients into the right kind of focused action.

2. **Start noting events of significance in your life**. Take time to jot down five to ten key events that come to mind. Don't second guess. Once you write these down, more will start coming to mind spontaneously.

3. **Pick events that include positive emotions** later on in the story, even if the beginning is challenging.

To develop greater fluency with the language of emotions, which is essential to all storytelling, please read Chapter 6: 'The Heart of the Matter: A New Interpretation of Emotions' by Dan Newby.

---

4. **Include difficulties** because life is full of hurdles, unexpected obstacles, and problems, whether we want to call them 'challenges' or something else. Life can be hard at times, and our clients know that.

5. **End on a positive note**. Even though your story will include obstacles and hurdles, it should finish with a deep insight, better results or insightful learning.

Inspiration for stories and metaphors

Often coaches wonder where they can get stories and metaphors from and if they have to come from the client. While it is a good idea to include symbols from the client's problem and outcome, there are strong advantages to using your own metaphors: you know these intimately, are emotionally connected to them and are clear on the sequence of events. It is worth sitting down and taking some time to think of five to ten times in your life when something of significance happened. I pick times I had adventures, achieved something, overcame the odds, came back from something challenging or happy childhood memories:

- Getting a swimming honours award when I was 11 years old
- Retrieving the ring for my dad's friend from the floor of the Indian Ocean
- Travelling around Italy with my sister while studying at the University of Bologna
- Getting a place at university after moving back to the UK from Tanzania
- Meeting my wife at a friend's party
- My life experiences since I became a dad
- Running various half marathons around the UK – and the sense of achievement completing my first one when I had never run 13 miles before.

You are already a natural storyteller because that is how we bond socially. When the pressure is off, we tell people all sorts of stories about our lives as a way to connect:

- Moving house
- Our journey to meet friends and what happened on the way
- Holiday experiences
- Achievements like getting a new job
- Trips abroad
- Interesting or unusual things that happened to colleagues, friends, and family
- Surprise at excellent (or disappointing) customer service.

With close friends we open up and tell those more personal stories:

- First love
- The story of how we met our partner
- Getting a job after feeling anxious
- Going through a difficult life experience and ending up on top.

All of these are stories (metaphors), and we habitually tell them with zero pressure (as a storyteller) because doing so is as natural as breathing.

If telling a story does not sit well with you because it feels too personal, you can still use it by translating the metaphor into the third person. I could, for instance, change my diving story in the following ways:

- *A person went diving one day…*
- *A friend went diving one day…*
- *A woman took a journey out to sea…*
- *Years ago, a wise man took his son on a journey…*

Other sources of metaphors include movies, TV shows and books that resonate deeply with you. As a result, it is simple to generate a never-ending list of fascinating stories with the potential to impact clients positively.

Client success metaphors

One of my favourite ways to use metaphors in coaching is to tell clients a story about another successful client.

Imagine this: you have a consultation with a prospective coaching client, or you are actually in a live session with an existing client and have an intervention in mind for them. Rather than do a coaching intervention 'cold,' you decide to prime the client for success by saying, *A while back, I had a client who was having this difficulty. We did this process that I think you would enjoy.* You then tell them the story (metaphor) which outlines the successful states, stages, and emotions the client went through – all the way to a successful coaching conclusion!

> My client had a fear of presenting in public. It had been getting worse for several years. He ran a successful business and was a well-established and popular musician. He loved his work and everyone who sang with him. He was a great guy and very encouraging to other performers, even if they didn't start with any 'natural ability,' as long as they were committed to doing the work to deliver the best performance they could. He liked people, yet became aware he was starting to feel increasingly anxious socially. He couldn't make sense of it, consciously. Now he realised that he was suffering from a kind of social anxiety around people because of 'chronic over-thinking' and this was spilling over into other areas, such as performing. And he knew it would be

disastrous if he didn't get it handled. So he came to see me. I explained that the first thing I do is ask all new coaching clients to fill out a detailed application form, so I can tailor their sessions and get all the facts. I also tell them that I will be working with their unconscious mind, which is the seat of their emotions and creativity. So he came along, and he was really motivated to change. He was totally focused. He was very patient answering all my questions, and, at one point, I did some simple closed eye processes that helped him gain even greater focus and control over his thoughts. He was amazed at how trying something new for a few moments could create such impact. He said, 'I didn't expect to be able to do that so quickly.' He had this big grin on his face and went, 'I already feel like I can do this! That is weird.'

Not only will telling stories about successful clients help a person transform, but this is deeply convincing for prospective clients because it adds value when prospective clients realise that coaching works. The problem is that if you consciously say, 'coaching is great' it has less impact. When you tell the story (metaphor) of how someone changed thanks to coaching, then you build firm belief through implication.

This is elegant and effective because it allows the coach to prime their client for success – whatever intervention or process they decide to do next. They told a metaphor and influenced their client without them even knowing it!

Coaching insights and summary

Metaphors allow coaches to leverage their personal life experiences as vehicles for transformation in clients. Sharing resourceful chains of emotions creates a kind of sympathetic resonance where the client experiences to some degree what the coach is experiencing. Consider this brief metaphor:

> I went for a run one lunchtime while training for a half marathon. This particular day, I surprised myself with how far I could jog. I felt light, happy and strong with no sign of needing to slow down. I was in the zone. My energy was so high that it seemed like I could go on forever – and I went further than I'd ever been before.

The positive energy of 'being surprised once you get going and take action' is hugely beneficial because I get to leverage that (i.e. recreate the same emotion and feeling): I have it on tap every time I narrate that story. I get to tell the client implicitly, *Get going and you will be amazed at what you can do and how much energy you have to succeed* without actually having to say those words. That is the power of metaphor!

Coaching in action

Theory

Minds work by building associations: metaphor is one expression of this. Change the metaphor, and you change the meaning of an experience. In this way, metaphors function as Deep Reframes.

Action

A simple way to begin introducing metaphors naturally into coaching sessions is to start telling clients 'success metaphors' about other clients. Start collecting positive experiences that clients have and share them with other clients (maintain privacy by keeping it general, e.g. 'A client I had once…'):

1. Elicit coaching problem in one context

2. Ask your client what their outcome is

3. Pick a story about a different client where (i) they had a problem and felt stuck; (ii) they had some insight or shift in perspective; (iii) they felt a change in emotion, which caused them to take different actions and (iv) there was a positive end result

4. Deliver the metaphor. 'I had a client once who had a similar problem. No matter what they tried, x and y happened to them. Things were looking dire....'

Once you are comfortable doing this, start introducing success metaphors into your consultations with prospective clients and organisations, and see the magic happen!

~

Connect with the Author

Thank you for taking time to read this chapter. If you are feeling excited about the possibilities of using stories for coaching and in your day-to-day life, then congratulations! As you start using metaphor in coaching, you are welcome to share your experiences of applying the techniques, tools and strategies in this chapter. To find out more, connect and fully explore further creative methods for generating lasting change for you or your organisation please contact me at richard@richardhaggerty. co.uk or visit www.RichardHaggerty.co.uk

III

THE EMOTIONS

Covered in this section

Emotions are an undeniable part of every human being's make up yet we tend to overlook their importance. More and more we are waking up to the vital role emotions play in our thinking and behaviour. They are no longer something we can deny or ignore if we want to achieve better results.

In the following two chapters, we share an interpretation of emotions that is practical and even logical. In the first chapter, we explain what emotions are and how they relate to listening, thinking and identity. In the second, we present a model of coaching that puts emotions at the centre of the action.

Chapter 6: The Heart of the Matter: A New Interpretation of Emotions
Dan Newby

Dan leads us to a deeper appreciation of emotions as a primary tool for coaching. What moves us to action is the link between our thoughts and actions. It is here where the emotions power us to take action, or not. 'E' represents the energy needed to achieve 'MOTION,' that moves us forwards into taking actions. This new area of coaching takes us even deeper into the drivers of action as they are experienced by our clients, and how we can work most effectively with these.

Chapter 7: Getting to the Heart of the Matter: Emotions-Centred Coaching
Dan Newby

Dan shares with us how to introduce emotions and moods into our coaching. His unique Six Step model includes language, conversation, emotions and the whole body in creating new practices for the client to achieve sustainable change and results. Dan also gives us six case studies for emotions that may be interfering with the client's effectiveness, so that we can clearly understand how to work with and integrate them into our own coaching practice.

CHAPTER 6

THE HEART OF THE MATTER

A New Interpretation of Emotions

Dan Newby

Emotions are a non-discretionary part of every human being; however, unlike intellect, we've mostly left their development to chance.

Covered in this chapter
- The purpose, importance and interpretation of emotions in coaching
- The relationship between emotions and moods, and the difference between them
- Three properties every emotion has and things that are 'not quite' emotions
- Emotional clusters and how similar emotions get mislabelled
- The value of suggesting possible emotions in coaching
- The 7 filters to focus and enhance listening skills when coaching to emotions

---

With a grimace that betrayed exasperation his thoughts spilled out, 'I wish I wasn't so impatient! I can't tell you how often it gets in my way and, to be honest, I don't like that about myself.' His self-judgement and confusion were clear.

As coaches, this type of story is familiar: a client, dissatisfied with the way they behave; who believes they don't have the power to change. As coaches, we know to listen into the story for the beliefs that are holding our client captive. In this case, we could challenge the client's belief that they are fixed in their way of thinking to help them explore alternatives from the perspective of language. For a lot of coaches that would be a typical approach, but our investigation can go deeper. If we go beneath the level of master assessments or beliefs, we can find an entire world of coaching possibilities in emotions.

A NEW VIEW OF EMOTIONS

When I use the word 'emotion,' it probably means something different than the way you understand it. The vast majority of coaches I know have learned to intervene from the perspective of language. This is a natural starting point for creating investigative conversations because of our comfort and familiarity with language. Language is the tool of reason, our cognitive interface. We think, speak, listen, read and write in language. It is a fantastic tool for putting things in order, grouping them, separating them and seeing the relationship between or among them. For all its power, however, it doesn't move us. What moves us – the link between our thoughts and actions – is emotions. Look at the etymology of the word emotion, and you'll see that it originally meant 'to move out,' 'that which moves us' or 'that which puts us in action.'

I take this interpretation of emotions literally. If we did not have emotions we would not, could not, leverage our intellect, reason and logic to act. We would be unable to do anything because there would be no 'fuel for action.' This interpretation is a change from the one we've operated out of for several centuries. We have come to see emotions as opposing logic rather than a collaborator to it. We've believed emotions get in the way of clear thinking rather than understanding that emotions are part of the way we think; change the emotion, change the thought. We've seen emotions as random, unpredictable and annoying. In fact, emotions have a logical, even mechanical, structure and are entirely predictable. What is not predictable are the events that trigger them, but emotions themselves are consistent. We have a distrustful relationship with emotions which we can reconsider if we adopt a new understanding of them.

Redefining emotions

There is a wealth of information and many clues for us as coaches when we are emotionally literate, or even better, emotionally fluent. That doesn't only mean we are aware of emotional intelligence and understand it theoretically but that we are practitioners. Our collective understanding of emotions is growing every day. We are beginning to accept emotions as a centre of intelligence. We now know that emotions are also a domain of learning and it is starting to dawn on us that they might be as important as our intellectual capacity. This is a far cry from the ways we have regarded, or rather, disregarded, emotions until recently. To frame this new interpretation of emotions, consider the following:

- Emotions are simply 'the energy that moves us': There is no universal definition of what constitutes an emotion so we must choose an interpretation.
- There is no definitive list of emotions: I have identified more than 200. You can develop your vocabulary of emotions and help clients develop theirs.
- Emotions are interpretations: Emotions cannot be seen directly and are interpreted from a person's language and body. Because of this, we cannot put a single definition on them, but we can agree on a precise interpretation.

- Emotions and thoughts are co-creative: what we think generates emotions; emotions generate what we think.
- Emotions are nondiscretionary; every human is an emotional being: Just as our heart beating is not something we choose, so it is with emotions.
- We are always in one or more emotions: just as our body never stops its work and our brains never stop processing, our emotions also never stop.
- Emotions are a domain of learning and thus of knowledge and wisdom.
- Emotions are contagious: we communicate through the energy of emotions which is called limbic resonance.
- Emotions are not inherently 'good' or 'bad': although we have assessments and judgements of emotions, a more useful question about an emotion is 'whether it is serving us at this moment, or not?'
- Emotions are logical: every emotion gives us information, has an impulse and a purpose. For me, these are the criteria that establish something as an emotion.
- We learn emotions through immersion over time: this is different from cognitive learning which occurs almost instantly through insight.
- We do not control our emotions but can learn to navigate them and use them as a tool.

The elements of this interpretation collectively give us an enormously valuable tool for understanding ourselves and our clients and can be used in coaching to significant effect.

Demystifying emotions

Humans have had many interpretations of emotions over the millennia. Every culture has developed its own way of understanding them. In some, they have been related to the whims of the gods (or devil) and in others the balance of bile in the digestive tract or other forces. Our current interpretation of emotions might be thought of as psychological. We've placed emotions within the purview of psychology and, in many ways, put them off limits to other interpretations. One outcome of this is that when we are challenged by something in the emotional domain we believe we need to seek out a professional to understand and resolve it. This takes emotions out of the domain of learning and makes them unavailable as a source of daily understanding and support. It means we have not considered them as something we can intentionally learn and teach as we do with other disciplines such as mathematics or literature. The idea of limiting emotional investigation and learning to a single profession is a bit like restricting mathematics only to mathematicians. While we may not use trigonometry daily, we certainly use other maths skills in every part of our lives. The question I would pose is, why don't we do the same with emotions?

If emotions are 'the energy that moves us' and if every human has emotions, it seems that they are an essential area of competence for each of us to live consciously and productively. As coaches, the universality of emotions is a wonderful gift. It means that even when we don't share the same points of reference as our clients, we know that they have emotions and that emotions are determining all they do. That assurance gives us a basis to work across cultures, languages and intergenerationally.

If we think about our relationship with language, we consider it normal and common sense that most people can read and write. When we are seated at a restaurant, the server does not ask us if we are literate before handing us a menu. He or she assumes we can read because it is 'common sense;' it is the standard. Emotions, however, are still considered awkward and uncomfortable because they lack the 'normalcy' that language has obtained. That normalcy is the goal of emotional literacy. When we believe that emotions are 'just part of being human' in the same way as breathing, sleeping and eating, we will quit seeing them as awkward or 'in the way.' When we get to that point, emotions become a tool we can use daily and, as coaches, can employ with our clients as easily and naturally as we do asking questions.

Emotions and moods

We often use the words 'emotion' and 'mood' interchangeably. While they both are part of the emotional domain, there are significant differences, and they support us in different ways. Every emotion is triggered by an event. Someone runs into us with their shopping cart, and it triggers annoyance or irritation. Someone gives us a gift, and it triggers delight. A thought, a bodily sensation or an experience can be the origin. Moods are not triggered, and they are the lens through which we interpret events. If we are in the mood of fear, everything looks dangerous; in gratitude, everything is a gift.

While there is no absolute rule regarding the duration of an emotion or mood, experience tells us that emotions come and go much faster than moods. An emotion might last a fraction of a second to a few hours. It will shift when a new experience triggers a different emotion. After a few hours, it takes considerable energy to maintain an emotion. As children, we sometimes tell people we'll be mad at them forever but within a few minutes have moved to other emotions. As adults, we do the same, although perhaps not as publicly. Moods, by contrast, are the background emotional energy we live in. They could last for a day, week, year or lifetime. A helpful analogy is that moods are like the deep water in the ocean; there are currents, but they move slowly. Emotions are like the surface of the water, at times calm and at other times choppy or rough. We will tend to revert to our by-default mood when the stimulation of emotions stops. In quiet, reflective times it is easier to see the mood in which we live.

The value of this distinction in coaching is that it means we have two emotional territories to explore. The exploration of moods helps us determine the lens through which the client sees and interprets the world. A client in the mood of ambition sees possibilities and is energised to go after them whereas one in the mood of resignation sees a world that does not have possibilities. This is essential because the mood determines the world that is seen. As a coach we might see dozens of possibilities for our client but as long as they remain in the mood of resignation those possibilities do not exist for them. It isn't that they do not *want* to see them; it is that they *cannot* see them. In this case, helping the client shift their mood is the starting point.

The key to working with emotions is the ability to distinguish between them, and hear their message precisely. For coaches to learn this, we must understand the underlying story of each emotion, its predisposition or impulse, and its purpose. Knowing these three allows us to differentiate which emotion is driving our client and producing their challenge. From there helping them understand the emotion they are experiencing and to choose a more useful emotion is a typical path.

Deconstructing emotions

My claim that emotions are logical stems from the fact that each can be seen to have a predictable, even mechanical, structure. The best way to see this is through what is sometimes called linguistic deconstruction of emotions.

According to this interpretation, every emotion has three properties:

- It gives us information or 'tells us a story'
- It has an impulse or predisposition
- It has a purpose or takes care of us in some way.

How emotions inform us

Let's take the emotion of sadness. We may feel sad because our dog ran away, someone close to us passed away, or a friend moves across the country. These are personal experiences that can trigger sadness, but they have a common underlying or foundational story. That story is, 'I've lost something I care about.' Simply losing something is not enough to provoke sadness. Imagine your dog ran away, but it wasn't a dog you liked. That would not provoke sadness, and you might even be happy the dog left. The 'something lost' must be something you cared about, or you will not feel sad. This means that sadness is predictable and also that when we feel sad, we can know we've lost something we care about even if we can't identify it.

Every emotion has an impulse or predisposition

Every emotion has a predisposition or 'wants us to behave in a specific way.' In sadness, we have the impulse to withdraw and grieve. In the case of our dog running away, we may cry or grieve our loss by being alone and reflective. We may postpone the impulse because of our socialisation or other commitments, but it is what we feel like doing. Each emotion has its characteristic predisposition. In resentment we want to 'get even for what we believe is unfair' and in joy, we feel like celebrating. So, if we notice how we are moved or how we are inclined to behave it is an indicator of the emotion we are experiencing.

Every emotion has a purpose

Third, all emotions have a purpose. They do not appear randomly or capriciously. The purpose of fear is to keep us safe, of ambition to go after opportunities. When I say that emotions are not 'good' or 'bad,' it is because every emotion takes care of us in some way. The sadness we feel when our dog went missing tells us what we care about.

Emotions either serve us in the moment, or they do not. In terms of purpose, the most important thing we can evaluate is what emotion will best help us navigate our current situation.

Decoding emotions

Having these deconstructions fluidly available is of enormous value to a coach. The moment our client starts a story about their employees being too slow we know they are probably experiencing frustration. If they say they feel like celebrating the team's success, the client is most likely experiencing joy, and if they want to tell others about that success, it is probably pride. As a coach what this means is that we do not need to listen to long stories or explanations to understand the client's emotional situation. We can understand what is moving or motivating him / her in just a sentence or two. We will also know how he or she is likely to react. We get an immediate insight into our client's way of being that otherwise is unavailable. These deconstructions can also help our client understand his / her team, boss or peers if we share them. Lastly, knowing these allows us as coaches to understand our own emotional choreography and choose appropriate responses. Imagine we feel frustration working with a client. Some of us would recoil because we believe we 'shouldn't' be frustrated with a client because we judge it to be disrespectful. However, if we understand that frustration means we believe it should be going faster or with less effort and that it prompts us to look for alternatives, we can see frustration as a beneficial emotion in coaching.

Emotional clusters

There are groups of emotions that often get confused or conflated. Empathy, sympathy, compassion and pity are examples. The confusion can occur because the emotions tend to show up in similar circumstances or because they feel similar somatically. I call these 'clusters of emotions' likening them to a cluster of grapes; distinct but hanging together. As we develop our understanding of individual emotions, it is beneficial to identify the other emotions with which they may be clustered.

Cluster 1: Anger, resentment and frustration
Many times, a client will say they feel angry. If we take their statement at face value, we will begin coaching to the anger. Anger, however, is often confused with frustration or resentment. In anger, their story will be connected with injustice. Someone did something to them that was morally wrong or unjust. Frustration is the story 'it shouldn't be this difficult' or 'it shouldn't take this long' and has nothing to do with injustice when seen in isolation. Resentment is the story that 'it shouldn't be this way' and has to do with unfairness. If we clearly identify the emotion at the centre of the client's challenge or breakdown it gives us a reliable direction for our coaching.

Cluster 2: Fear, anxiety and doubt
Another cluster to be aware of is fear, anxiety and doubt. I find that when a client says they feel fear, it is wise to have a conversation about the three before deciding on a coaching path. Fear means we believe something may harm us and we can identify it. 'I fear getting hit by a bus.' In the case of fear,

because we can identify the source of the danger, we can make a plan to manage it. Anxiety occurs when we believe something may harm us, but we are unclear of the source of danger. In anxiety, we fall into a circular conversation called worry. Because we can't name the danger, we cannot break out of the worry. Doubt is very different from the other two, and it shows up when we are entering a new domain. When we drive to a new place, cook a new recipe or give our first presentation to a large group, doubt is predictable because we are in unknown territory. Doubt's purpose is to call our attention to preparation and not assume 'we already know.' These three emotions tend to be confused because they occur when we are facing an unknown future, and they feel similar somatically.

Cluster 3: Excitement, ambition and enthusiasm
These three emotions are all considered desirable emotions, but they serve different purposes. Excitement is a high level of energy that produces the desire for more excitement. In ambition, we see possibilities and want to take advantage of them. Enthusiasm is the emotion that connects us with a larger purpose and gives us energy to continue even when we may never see the final outcome. When a coach understands these three distinctly, he or she may find that a leader has 'burnt out' on ambition but may get refuelled by enthusiasm or may need some excitement to get reconnected with ambition. Each is a distinct tool.

Distinguishing which emotion is driving the client's concern is essential to choosing an effective coaching direction.

'Not quite emotions'

What defines something as an emotion for me is that it has the three aspects of story, impulse and purpose. It is essential that it has a single underlying story. If it does not then, in my interpretation, it is not an emotion, it may, however, be an emotional indicator or 'not quite an emotion.' A good example is overwhelm. A client may say he or she is 'overwhelmed' believing they are sharing their emotion. However, since we can be overwhelmed by many things – unexpectedly inheriting a million dollars, exhaustion, joy, anguish – I consider it an emotional indicator. Useful but not definitive. Just as with emotional clusters this is important because to work with emotions we need precision.

Coaching strategy: suggesting possibilities
Other 'not quite emotions' common in coaching conversations are stressed, burnt out, exhausted, stuck, detached, positive, negative or upbeat. They all tend to be either an expression of how our body is feeling, or a metaphor or analogy. As a coach, investigating what emotions the client is experiencing and which they are trying to articulate is essential. If not, we will enter a circular conversation that will not go deep enough to address the breakdown. The coaching strategy is to ask the client what other word they would use to describe their experience and to name an emotion if possible. When they can't come up with a name, a methodology that is effective is to name an emotion you think they might be experiencing and let them react. I've observed that humans tend to know what they don't want even when they can't say what they do want. So, when we offer the client an emotion that does not resonate, their response will be something like, 'No, it isn't that, it is more like "…"'. That takes us a step closer to identifying the emotion precisely.

The 7 filters

In coaching interventions, there are 7 filters we can use to focus our listening. They are:

1. Not good or bad
2. Time orientation
3. Direction of reference
4. Drama vs emotions
5. Reacting vs responding
6. Emotional duality
7. Listening for what is said and what is not.

Not good or bad
Humans everywhere I've worked share the habit of categorising emotions into two baskets labelled 'good emotions' and 'bad emotions.' We generally throw anger, jealousy, arrogance, greed, frustration and resignation, among others, into the 'bad' basket and love, enthusiasm, generosity, joy, compassion and hope into the 'good' basket. The placement of some, like ambition and passion, often depends on the cultural context.

While there is nothing fundamentally incorrect about identifying emotions in this way it does have a consequence. The consequence is that we tend to avoid the 'bad' emotions and pursue the 'good' emotions. We tend to ignore the 'bad' emotions and thereby miss their benefit. We don't listen to or reflect on what they are telling us, and we don't allow ourselves to be in the experience of them. We often hastily try to change them or distract ourselves from them. A helpful distinction is that there are, of course, emotions that 'feel bad,' meaning we don't enjoy the sensation they bring, but we tend to confuse that with believing the emotions itself is 'bad.' The same goes for emotions that have a pleasant feeling associated with them.

CASE STUDY: REDEFINING GUILT

Let's take the example of guilt. For most of us, the emotion of guilt goes in the 'bad' basket, and we don't enjoy the way it feels. Our by-default or habitual way of relating to guilt is often trying to 'get over it' as quickly as possible. This is something I regularly find in my coaching. I recall a client who had promised at the conclusion of one session to read a paper I'd written in preparation for our subsequent conversation. When he came to the next session, the first thing he said was that he felt guilty because he hadn't read the paper. To his surprise, my response was, 'That's great!' I shared that his guilt told me that he was aware of his commitments and took them seriously. Where he saw a weakness, I saw a strength and our different ways of seeing the situation came from our individual interpretations of the meaning of guilt.

Since there are no universal definitions of emotions, we can and must choose an interpretation. When we want to use our interpretation with others, we need to agree on a shared interpretation. When we don't, we are in different conversations.

Deconstructing guilt will show us:

- Story: 'I'm aware I've broken my personal values.'
- Impulse: To chastise or punish ourselves
- Purpose: To remind us of / clarify our personal values

If, as we usually do, we focus on chastising ourselves we may miss the tremendous importance of guilt's purpose. Particularly in coaching conversations, is it more useful to adopt the question, 'Is this emotion serving me or not serving me in this moment?' Fear serves us by keeping us safe and sometimes gets in our way by preventing us from doing things we would like to do. Anger serves us by showing what we believe to be unjust but, in anger, we can also damage relationships or hurt others. This idea applies to all emotions, and developing an understanding of each emotion in this way is a key component of emotional literacy.

Time orientation

Emotions have a time orientation which can help us enormously as coaches. Imagine a client who says he has a strong desire to create his own business but is frustrated because he isn't taking steps to make his vision a reality. You notice that he often talks about a relationship that ended because his partner believed it wasn't sustainable. He also talks about how he'd like to go back to the island where he lived with his partner and how much he misses it. From the emotional perspective, your client is living in two eras. His ambition and enthusiasm are about the future and his nostalgia regarding his relationship is about the past. As a coach, it is useful to be able to deconstruct this client's emotions but the most important aspect to understand is the time orientation of them. Quite simply he is more committed to his past than his future. I often find that clients are not aware of this and are confused why they cannot move forward. The move I used with this client was inviting him to declare acceptance, an emotion rooted in the present, that the relationship was over and there was, in fact, no 'going back.' Doing that moved him into the present from which the future was just one step rather than two.

Direction of reference

Many emotions have a direction of reference. Fear, anxiety and doubt are about ourselves, while love, service and generosity are about others. Some emotions such as awe and faith refer to the unknowable or immaterial, while others, such as certainty and trust are about the known. Like time orientation, this is a useful thing to understand and look for in the emotions of our clients. We will have clients who are anxious or doubtful before a presentation or conversation. If we can help them see that those emotions exist to take care of themselves and are self-referential, it is often easy for them to find an emotion that is other-referential and puts their focus on others. In this case, they might feel doubt because they've never given a presentation to such a large audience and the shift could come if they begin to imagine the experience they want to create for that audience. Simply shifting to an emotion with a different direction of reference can alter the client's attention and concern.

A similar strategy, involving what is known and unknown, can be effective for a client who is bored with their work. Boredom means we 'don't see anything of value to us' in a situation. By inviting your client to seek out activities that trigger wonder – which is 'to enjoy the experience even though we don't understand them' – they will discover aspects of life they don't currently see.

Drama vs emotions
I've heard people speak about other cultures as 'emotional' or 'not emotional.' Italians are often credited with being very emotional, and Canadians are not. The difference I would suggest is that those from one culture are more *dramatic* than the other, but having worked with both Canadians and Italians I can report that both have a full range of emotions. This is something we often confuse. Emotions are the energy that moves us while drama is the level of animation with which we express the emotion. Some emotions have a higher level of energy than others: sadness vs enthusiasm, for instance – but the overall range of expression can be thought of as drama.

This level of animation can be culturally driven like the example above, but individual constitution and experiences along with the learning from our families seem to be the other main drivers. This drama, or level of animation, should not be confused with emotional knowing. One may be more dramatic expressing their emotions, but that does not mean they understand them better or can leverage them as a tool more effectively than others. As a coach, it is valuable to recognise and pay attention to this difference. It is easy to get drawn in by the energy of a client's emotions and lose sight of the information they are offering or their purpose for showing up in that situation. When a client learns the difference, it may change the way they understand themselves in the emotional domain. They may realise that they are emotional beings and have emotions but have learned it was safer or more appropriate not to express them. At that point, they can make a choice about the level of expression that would best serve them and their relationships.

Reacting vs responding
Every emotion makes us react in a specific way. Our reactions tend to be grouped into fight, flight, freeze or submit and these are common to most of us. We cannot avoid these reactions, but we can learn to anticipate and navigate them differently.

In some cases that may take care of the situation to our satisfaction, but, in other cases, it may not. Anger tells us we are experiencing something we consider 'unjust' or morally wrong. Imagine we see someone hitting a child. It will provoke anger in us if we believe it is unjust. Our reaction may be to hit or punish the person responsible, but this may not be the most effective long-term solution. In a situation like this, being able to respond is valuable. Reaction is instant and automatic; response comes after time and reflection and is a conscious choice. In the case cited, an effective response might be to report the parent to authorities, have a conversation with their spouse or talk with them directly at another time.

We have a number of possible strategies for moving from reaction to response. Counting to ten is one we commonly suggest to others even if we don't practise it. Breath is a key and being able to breathe in a way that stimulates our parasympathetic system usually helps a great deal. Meditation, running, a good sleep or a conversation with a committed listener are all ways to create the time and reflection to move to response.

Emotional duality

As coaches, we are always in an emotional duality. We are humans and thus experiencing emotions and moods constantly and, at the same time, we are observing and working with our clients' moods and emotions. We need to develop the capacity to remain aware of both sets of emotions to coach effectively. This ability comes first by keeping front of mind the questions, 'What emotion am I hearing or seeing in my client?' and 'What emotion am I noticing in myself?'

One tremendous benefit of observing our emotions while we are coaching is that they suggest questions that are not based on logic and are not linear. When we trust our emotions and are willing to speak the questions that occur from that domain, we will find that our clients are surprised and that the questions lead them to breakthroughs that they couldn't have predicted. This requires us as coaches to develop our emotional fluency and to trust that no harm will come to the client if we ask the questions our emotions suggest to us. That takes time and experimentation.

Listening

A client I had came to his sessions in a wonderfully upbeat mood. He was always happy, seeing the good in everything and was full of gratitude. The contradiction I saw was that 'everything was good' yet he had requested coaching. It turned out that one of my client's breakdowns was his inability to admit that things weren't perfect, which meant he couldn't tell his boss bad news or challenge his team because he believed doing so constituted 'being negative.' Listening for what we don't hear is as important as listening for what we do.

What this interpretation of emotions allows us as coaches is to streamline the coaching process. Table 6.1 shows some ways this occurs when we use emotions-based listening:

Table 6.1: Decoding emotions

The story	When we are listening for the 'story' – for instance 'injustice' – we do not need to hear a lengthy explanation from our client. We do not need more information, only the key underlying story.
The impulse	The impulse quickly points to the emotion and clarifies it.
The purpose	Why is this emotion showing up now? What does the client make of it? How is it helpful?
Emotional cluster	Does the client have emotions confused or are they lacking clarity on what an emotion means?

'Not quite an emotion'?	Is the client trying to express their emotion but is not naming it precisely? What emotion are they trying to identify?
Judgement ('good' or 'bad' emotions)	Is the client shying away from an emotion because they judge it to be 'bad'?
Time orientation	In what era is our client living?
Direction of reference	Is the client caught up in emotions about themselves or others? Which orientation would be most helpful?
Drama vs emotions	Is your client sidetracked by their level of drama? How could they either raise or lower it to make their emotions more accessible and the emotional expression more effective?
Reacting vs responding	Would it be advantageous for your client to learn to respond to their emotions rather than react to them?

Duality	What information is our emotion giving us about the client or their challenge? What is our emotion prompting us to do?

Leveraging the coach's emotions

In the coaching relationship, both parties are moved by their emotions. As a coach, it is most useful to listen to and leverage the emotions that are provoked in you as you are coaching. For instance, frustration may show up, and our automatic response may be to think that, as a professional coach, we shouldn't feel that emotion. However, if we understand frustration to be telling us 'there must be a simpler or faster way' we will probably realise that the client is telling us the same circular story or is not progressing as they might. Sometimes sharing with the client what emotion is surfacing for us gives them an insight they would not have otherwise. Often, the emotional impact a client has on me as a coach is something they also trigger in others. This is often news to them.

Coaching insights and summary

In this chapter, we've constructed and explored a new interpretation of emotions and their role in human life. If we believe emotions are 'the energy that moves us' it is apparent that they are essential to coaching. It should be remembered that they are both 'the energy that moves us' and 'the energy that keeps us from moving.' When we consider emotions in coaching, we need to look for the emotions that are present and those we don't observe in our client and ourselves.

~

Connect with the Author

Thank you for sharing this time and exploration. I hope it has produced insights and connected with your work and life. To learn more about me, my work or ways to develop emotional literacy please visit my website www.schoolofemotions.world. You can reach me directly at dan@schoolofemotions.world

CHAPTER 7

GETTING TO THE HEART OF THE MATTER

Emotions-Centred Coaching

Dan Newby

Covered in this chapter
- The 6 steps to Emotions-Centred Coaching
- Emotions-Centred Coaching in action: case studies on impatience, responsibility and accountability, forgiveness, frustration, acceptance and joy

INTRODUCTION

In the previous chapter, I shared my interpretation of emotions and moods. Now you may be wondering how to seamlessly introduce emotions and moods into your coaching.

The pattern of Emotions-Centred Coaching, in general, is this:

1. Listen for the emotion connected to the client's challenge
2. Clarify how the client understands their emotion
3. Generate a shared interpretation
4. Investigate whether the emotion or mood is serving the client or not
5. Investigate what emotion or mood would be more useful
6. Design practices that allow the client to strengthen a more useful emotion / mood.

In terms of a model we could illustrate it as shown in Figure 7.1:

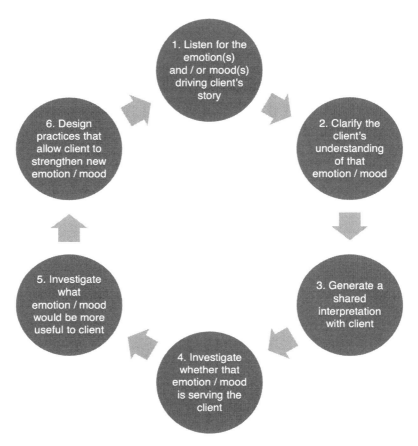

Figure 7.1: Emotions-Centred Coaching

While there will be many routes or loop-backs as the conversation unfolds, here are elements that are likely to occur in each part of the conversation:

Step 1: Listen for the emotion connected to the client's challenge

- Listening for emotion is different from our habitual way of listening. We are socially trained to listen to the story someone is telling. We are focused on information, history, relationships, timeline and ways in which the story 'adds up' to us or makes sense. All of those elements are important if we want to respond intelligibly. Listening for emotions means that when we hear the word 'should' we might connect it with the emotion of obligation and understand that the client believes they have no choice in the matter. We might also consider its connection with shame ('I have broken a standard of my community') or guilt ('I have broken my own standard'). If we hear the client say something is 'unfair' we are aware their emotion is likely resentment, and their impulse is to 'get even.' This type of listening requires us to listen 'into' the story to hear where it is coming from emotionally.

- This step is where a client may use 'not quite an emotion,' and you can help them name the root emotion that is challenging them. If they say they feel 'vulnerable' the exploration could be to see if that sensation is coming from the emotion of fear, anxiety, shame or lack of self-confidence (self-trust). Once they've identified the emotion precisely, you can begin to work with it.
- There may be more than one emotion, or you may find the client is confused by a cluster of emotions. An example is that when a client says they feel anxiety about an upcoming presentation it is often the case that they are experiencing anxiety, fear and doubt. The relevant question is 'which one is the barrier?' One way of exploring this is to help them distinguish what anxiety, fear and doubt mean and then to put percentages on them. *What % of what you are feeling is anxiety, what % is fear and what % is doubt?* They need to add up to 100%, of course. Clients are able to do this quite easily, and it helps them choose which emotion to focus on.

- It is valuable in this step to distinguish whether they are feeling an emotion or mood. Is this something that is connected with an event and is unique or is this a recurring pattern they often find themselves in?
- In this step, it is often useful to ask the client to connect the dots between their challenge and the emotion they've identified. This keeps the coach from making assumptions and also helps the client clarify what is happening for them. It has often occurred in my coaching sessions that the client sees a connection between their emotion and story that I do not. That is usually a beneficial thread to follow.

For more on the art of listening be sure to read Chapter 3: 'The Transformational Impact of Active Listening' by Colin D. Smith.

Step 2: Clarify how the client understands the emotion they have named

- Since we cannot see emotions directly, we have no choice but to work with interpretations. Your client has interpretations even if they are not aware what they are. They probably learned to name emotions mostly from imitating their parents, family and culture. Understanding what the emotion they've identified means to them is crucial for the coach. This is a place where assumptions are easy to make and will get the coach off track. I can recall in many sessions moving ahead with my own interpretation without asking the client's, and it has never been effective.
- Some clients have learned to attach the name of an emotion to an experience of a different emotion. It is not unusual for people to confuse jealousy with envy, or acceptance with resignation.

Step 3: Generate a shared interpretation

- As the coach, you will almost always have more understanding and distinctions of emotions than your client. That does not mean your interpretation is more correct than theirs. Generating a shared interpretation means you and the client assign the same meaning to the emotion along with its impulse. It goes without saying that a coach needs to bring humility and openness to this exploration.
- I do, at times, offer my clients possible interpretations or distinctions to see if they resonate and are useful. I find that sometimes a client's ability to articulate the emotion they are experiencing is lacking and offering them words to describe it is helpful. My observation is that a client will either say 'Yes, that describes what I am feeling' or 'No, that isn't quite it. It is more like....' In either case, we are able to move ahead in unison. It is important that the coach is not attached to the client's interpretation.

Step 4: Investigate whether the emotion / mood identified is serving the client

- This is another step where assumptions are not the coach's friend. We, as coaches, have assessments about emotions (helpful, not helpful) and we have judgements (good, bad, OK to have, not OK to have). If a client identifies their emotion as one that we have strong assessments or judgements about, it may lead us astray. What is important is to understand how the client understands the emotion and whether they see it as helpful or not.

Step 5: Investigate what emotion or mood would be more useful

- If a client has identified that fear is keeping them from moving forward, you might, together, identify courage as an emotion that would change their situation. In this situation, another possibility could be boldness. This is a conversation in which I sometimes suggest possible emotions and let the client react to them. I find that they know what will work even if they cannot articulate it.

Step 6: Design practices that allow the client to strengthen the more useful emotion / mood they have chosen

- Emotions do not change simply because we would like them to or wish they would. Change requires intervention in either our thinking or body. If someone wants to shift from the mood of entitlement to gratitude, it will probably require them to intervene in their thinking. The thoughts associated with entitlement are something like 'I deserve X because I am Y.' Gratitude can be generated by shifting their thought pattern to 'All that I am and have was a gift to me' (from God, the universe, the world, according to the client's beliefs). One story generates entitlement and the other gratitude.
- Another place we can intervene to shift emotions is the body. Since every emotion has a feeling, an impulse and a somatic disposition we have several possibilities. What most people refer to as 'feelings' are the sensations we experience in our body that 1) tell us we are experiencing

an emotion and 2) give us an indication which emotion it is. At the moment we feel the emotion we can put our attention on it and begin using the information it is providing. The moment we feel a knot in our stomach, we can begin to identify that we are in the neighbourhood of anxiety / fear / doubt. If we pay attention to the impulse or reaction, the emotion prompts us to get further information about which emotion we are experiencing. For instance, if we feel like lashing out at another person, we are probably in the area of anger or frustration. It may not tell us specifically which emotion we are experiencing but gets us closer. Finally, the way the emotion shapes our body – our disposition – gives us another level of information. Someone shuffling along with slumped shoulders and head hung low signals resignation, sadness or an emotion in that vein. Our client can shift their emotion (or mood) by becoming aware of and adjusting any of these three somatic aspects. Someone standing in resignation who straightens and lengthens their spine, raises their head, so their eyes take in the horizon and rolls their shoulders back will not be able to maintain the emotion of resignation.

Richard Haggerty explains in depth how we can help clients shift their perspective in Chapter 4: 'Breaking Free: Unlocking Doors with Deep Reframing.'

APPLICATION

CASE STUDY 1: IMPATIENCE

'I wish I wasn't so impatient. It is the biggest thing about myself I don't like, and I've never been able to control it.' That was the opening statement of my client. Her story sounds straight-forward enough, and she presented it to me with confidence.

Using the 6 steps of Emotions-Centred Coaching, the conversation went like this:

1. **Listen for the emotion.** She said her emotion was impatience, so there wasn't much listening required. Many times clients don't name an emotion when describing their challenge, so the coach needs to investigate.

2. **Clarify client's interpretation.** I wanted to be sure I understood what impatience meant to her so began by asking how she knew that was her emotion. Her response was 'that is what my parents always said.' This initial response didn't tell me how she understood impatience, but it did tell me where she learned her interpretation. When I asked the circumstances in which her parents said she was impatient she said, 'I would ask them to take us to the lake or a movie or camping, and whenever I asked those kinds of things they would say "stop being impatient".' As we explored, she shared that she was the eldest of four children. She was obviously energetic and outgoing and always seemed to have ideas bubbling up.

3. **Generate a shared interpretation.** I asked her to consider the possibility that what she called impatience might be some other emotion. I asked her to list some other possibilities. On reflection,

she said it might be enthusiasm, excitement or even ambition. Then she thought of exuberance. We talked about what each of those meant and how they feel somatically. In the end, she decided that exuberance, meaning 'Life is abundant, and I want to participate,' was it.

4. **Investigate whether the emotion is serving.** My client decided that seeing herself as impatient was not helpful and it wasn't an accurate representation of her dominant emotion.

5. **Explore which emotion will serve better.** She decided that from then on she was going to think of herself as exuberant rather than impatient. She acknowledged that she was, at times, impatient but that wasn't the emotion she experienced most.

6. **Design a practice.** My client decided that the most immediate thing she could do was change her language. She wouldn't refer to herself anymore as impatient and would start describing herself as exuberant. If necessary, she would explain it to people so that they would understand her energy. She also said she decided that there would be times to 'dial back' her exuberance because other people in her life might, like her parents, interpret her energy as impatience. Finally, she decided to write her autobiography from the perspective of exuberance to reframe all the stories she had about herself related to impatience.

For me, this was a lovely coaching conversation and had an outcome that was fluid and impactful. The synopsis I've presented took place over three coaching sessions with time for her to reflect in between. You'll notice that we didn't spend much time trying to figure out what her parents intended by using the word 'impatient.' We didn't need to have an absolute definition of any of the emotions but only needed to agree on what they meant and what actions they provoked for the sake of the conversation. I noticed a significant shift in the client's body when she let go of the idea that she was impatient. She relaxed and began to enjoy the energy of exuberance. In my words, I would say she was more 'coherent' as a human being because her language, emotions, and body were more aligned.

CASE STUDY 2: RESPONSIBILITY AND ACCOUNTABILITY

This client was country director of a multinational that managed construction of large infrastructure projects. The concern that provoked his desire for coaching was his doubt that he was suitable for the job even though he had been in it for a decade.

1. **Listen for the emotion of the client.** Our coaching began with a discussion of why he thought he might not be qualified. One thing he said caught my attention which was, 'I want to be able to take a stand, but I am always going around making sure everyone is happy.' For me, this statement pointed to several possible emotions. One was dignity which is the emotion connected to the belief that 'we are a legitimate human being and can take a stand for what we believe.' When we lack dignity, we do not have access to indignance which allows us to defend our boundaries. Another emotion his statement suggested was guilt which occurs when we act in ways out of alignment with our values.

2. **Clarify client's interpretation.** As we explored in the first few sessions, my client shared specific situations he was challenged by. The pattern emerged that his habit was to take responsibility for things outside of his control. He was not clear on the distinction between responsibility and accountability.

3. **Generate a shared interpretation.** We discussed what these two emotions meant and agreed that responsibility meant that one 'took ownership' of a situation and accountability meant one was 'answerable' for something. My client sorted through situations he was challenged by and began to see that he was accountable for running the business and taking actions when needed, but he was not responsible for specific ways his team or clients behaved.

4. **Investigate whether the emotion is serving the client.** This insight helped him see why he couldn't take a stand and why he felt guilty. His internal value was that people are responsible for the actions they take, but when he assumed that responsibility for his clients he was violating his own standard. He also saw that his hard work at 'being nice so that everyone was happy' worked against holding his team responsible for their work.

5. **Explore which emotion will serve the client better.** The answer to this had already emerged, and the client determined that acting from accountability would help resolve the situation while at the same time strengthening his dignity and lessening his guilt.

6. **Design a practice.** The practice the client designed was nothing more complicated than keeping the two words accountability and responsibility in front of him visually in several ways and making time to reflect on his decisions and conversations. He chose to let responsibility be the emotion that guided his work.

One question that came up in my coaching conversations with this client was whether accountability and responsibility are emotions or behaviours. Since there is not a universal list of emotions, the approach I take is that if I can identify the three aspects – story, impulse and purpose – I can consider it an emotion. That does not mean it is not also a behaviour, or in other cases a belief or value. My thought is that responsible behaviour – taking ownership – is provoked by an emotion so for the sake of the coaching conversation let's think about that emotion as responsibility. Likewise with accountability.

CASE STUDY 3: FORGIVENESS

I often find that the interpretation of an emotion a client has grown up with can be the barrier they are facing. I'm thinking of an example of a retired business leader who told me he was haunted by an incident that occurred when he was CEO. He shared that, during a difficult financial period, he had pressed his production teams to produce more quickly. There was an accident, and a young worker suffered an injury that left him unable to walk. This leader said he had tried everything he could think of to stop blaming himself, but nothing had been successful.

1. **Listen for the emotion of the client.** I imagine because he had reflected on the occurrence often he was clear that he was caught in a cycle of self-blame and lack of forgiveness. There were sadness, regret and remorse as well but those weren't the emotions he was having difficulty with.

2. **Clarify client's interpretation.** When I asked the client to talk with me about forgiveness he replied that he was unable to forgive himself because he couldn't forget what had happened to the young worker. In that single statement, he shared that his interpretation of forgiveness required forgetting.

3. **Generate a shared interpretation.** We discussed whether it was possible to forgive without forgetting. There is a common expression, 'forgive and forget,' which we use without thinking about its meaning. If we do reflect on it, we'll see it isn't a very logical expression because if we've forgotten there is nothing to forgive. In the end, the client could see that he had been in a linguistic trap related to his emotions. How could he forget the young man who had been injured and if self-forgiveness required that it would never be possible?

4. **Investigate whether the emotion is serving the client.** The client concluded that he had been unable to forgive himself because of his understanding of forgiveness and so had been blaming himself for many years.

5. **Explore which emotion will serve better.** In other words, he concluded that he 'would remember what happened and his part in it but wouldn't continue to castigate himself.' He wouldn't use it against himself. What he could do was make amends as appropriate,

but his challenge was to change his understanding of forgiveness.

6. **Design a practice.** The practice the client chose was intervening in his story or thoughts. Whenever he would begin the internal conversation loop that was part of punishing himself, he would interrupt it and remind himself of his new interpretation of forgiveness.

Learning emotionally has similar steps to other learning. We start with attention then move to awareness, choice, practice and mastery. Emotions-Centred Coaching puts attention on the role of emotions in the client's challenge. The first 3 steps I have outlined mainly focus on creating awareness. Steps 4 and 5 lead to a commitment or choice, and step 6 begins practice. If a client continues to practice, competence and mastery will come.

CASE STUDY 4: FRUSTRATION

The client was a mid-level manager, new to having a team report to him. He was working very hard to fill his new role and was struggling. He told me he didn't understand why his team wasn't performing better. They knew what they were doing and could certainly produce more than they were.

1. **Listen for the emotion of the client.** My client told me the problem he had was his team's lack of results and because of that he was frustrated.

2. **Clarify client's interpretation.** I asked him to imagine that the emotion of frustration had the ability to speak. What would it say to him? He said it would probably say that his team was not working hard enough.

3. **Generate a shared interpretation.** We worked with the three elements of frustration a bit and concluded that frustration occurs when 'we believe something is taking too long or is more difficult than it needs to be.' That is what it is trying to tell us. Following that line of thought, I asked whether one's belief about how long things were taking was a fact or an opinion. He replied that in some cases it could be a fact but, in many cases, it was a feeling or an opinion. When I asked him where that opinion comes from, he said: 'probably previous experience.' *'Is it ever something we just make up?,'* I asked. He acknowledged that it could be. I was curious if the standard he was using was grounded or not, did it have a basis or was it simply an idea of how things should be? He said he knew things could be done faster because when he had the job, he was much more productive than they were now.

4. **Investigate whether the emotion is serving the client.** Having developed an understanding of frustration that was different than his previous one I asked him if he felt frustration was helping him as a manager or not. He said sometimes it helped get things done in the short term, but he was aware that it was also damaging his relationships with his clients.

5. **Explore which emotion will serve the client better.** *So, what emotion could take care of your relationships and help move towards increased productivity?,* I asked. 'Well, when I feel frustrated I get exasperated, I start blaming and quit looking for answers. I think what would really help is understanding why work is taking as long as it is,' he answered. He settled on curiosity as an emotion he'd like to cultivate.

6. **Design a practice.** As we discussed how he could make curiosity his default emotion, he realised that part of frustration was the belief that 'he already knew the answer.' Curiosity would require that he start with the acknowledgment that 'he didn't know.' His first commitment was to begin thinking differently. He would start internal conversations with 'I wonder why....' In his conversations with the client, he would also start with a statement that demonstrated curiosity such as 'help me understand' or 'I've been wondering.' He was clear this was something he would need to practise a lot since his belief that he knew the answer was immediate and strong.

Sometimes when we want to change our emotional habits, we focus on getting rid of the unwanted emotion. We feel fear and try to control or eliminate it. The problem with this approach is that we're still paying attention to the fear even if in a different way. Another approach is to choose an emotion that we'd like to replace the problematic one with, and focus on strengthening it. In the case of fear, we might choose courage which gives us the ability to act in the presence of fear. We might choose boldness which lets us step into action even when we feel fear. The result is that the challenging emotion begins to fade because we aren't putting attention on it any longer. In this case, the client chose curiosity to strengthen and allow his frustration to fade. It is a process that takes time but creates a sustained change.

CASE STUDY 5: ACCEPTANCE

A client came to me with the complaint that his wife travelled a lot for her work and he didn't like it. He said he 'accepted it was a necessity of her work, which she loved, but he wished she'd change jobs.'

1. **Listen for the emotion of the client.** The first thing I noticed about the client's story was that within a single sentence he was contradicting himself. He identified his emotion as acceptance, but his story betrayed him. When we are genuinely in acceptance, there is no 'but.' Acceptance simply means 'I acknowledge it is the way it is.'

2. **Clarify client's interpretation.** I shared what I saw as the contradiction, and he looked confused. As we explored he began to see that he wanted to accept the situation as a way to be supportive of his wife but that, in actuality, he wasn't in acceptance.

3. **Generate a shared interpretation.** Our conversation led to consideration of resignation, resentment, tolerance and other emotions that we sometimes confuse with acceptance. We agreed that resignation means 'I believe I can't change it,' resentment that 'it isn't fair' and tolerance that 'I'll put up with it.'

4. **Investigate whether the emotion is serving the client.** After consideration, the client said that his strongest emotion was resignation. He believed he couldn't change the situation, but he still didn't like it. He realised he had been feeling resignation but calling it acceptance. It might be true that he couldn't change the situation but believing he was in acceptance put him in a passive state.

5. **Explore which emotion will serve the client better.** Once he realised he was living in resignation, he could see why he hadn't talked with his wife about his feelings. He felt obligated to accept her travel because he loved her and wanted her to do work she enjoyed. He also was able to acknowledge that he didn't feel acceptance and that was OK.

6. **Design a practice.** In this case, the client decided that he didn't need a practice but only needed to take an action. That action was creating a conversation with his wife about how they could organise their lives so that she got to do the work she wanted and he got to have more time with her at home.

Acceptance is not a well-understood or popular emotion in some cultures. Some people understand acceptance as 'giving up' or 'submitting.' In action-oriented cultures, it is seen as passive and without value. Acceptance is sometimes confused with 'doing nothing,' but something significant occurs when we are able to accept a situation truly. We quit resisting or fighting against the situation, and that can allow us to move toward exploring new possibilities. Emotionally acceptance is similar to the 'you are here' marker on a tourist map. It doesn't really matter where you want to be until you know where you are. Once you acknowledge where you are you can look for ways to get to the location you desire.

CASE STUDY 6: JOY

The breakdown the client presented to me was that his team didn't seem motivated and given the targets the company had given him, he needed them to be. He said he was disappointed in them and, in all honesty, didn't have the energy to get them more engaged.

1. **Listen for the emotion of the client.** Listening to his story one emotion I heard clearly was disappointment. To me, that means he was expecting something to happen that didn't. That made sense as a secondary emotion but I was curious about his team and why they might not be more motivated. When I asked why he imagined his team was demotivated he said he thought it was probably because the work never stopped and when they did accomplish something it was not acknowledged by the company. It was just work and more work.

2. **Clarify client's interpretation.** It seemed clear that neither he nor his team did much celebrating. I asked him to tell me about the last time the team celebrated. He couldn't remember except to say that once in a while they got together at the bar for a drink. I asked what he knew about the emotion of 'gravitas.' He laughed, 'I didn't know that was an emotion. It sounds like gravity.' I told him he might know it better as seriousness and that it can be an emotion but also a mood. Someone who lives in the mood of seriousness or gravitas sees life as serious business, doesn't have lightness available and doesn't see the need for celebration. He told me that described his father exactly.

3. **Generate a shared interpretation.** 'So I know where I learned it,' he said. We talked more about gravitas and the emotions that it makes unavailable like joy and delight.

4. **Investigate whether the emotion is serving the client.** He decided that although it was important for the team to be serious about its work maybe, at times, it was counterproductive.

5. **Explore which emotion will serve the client.** This led to a conversation about the responsibilities of a leader and that the mood of the team was one of the responsibilities. He decided that what he probably needed to practise was joy even though he didn't think it was appropriate to tell his team. He could, however, plan ways to acknowledge their work and celebrate.

6. **Design a practice.** He chose, as his practice, to think of four ways he could introduce sincere acknowledgment and celebration to the team. He also committed to finding ways to celebrate personally as a way to strengthen joy as an emotion of his own.

We all know people who are very serious. Life is serious, business is serious, relationships are serious, making money is serious. Particularly in business, gravitas is an emotion or mood we value because we believe it leads to success. There are cultures that value serious and hard work and, for them, gravitas is the emotion that makes those possible. But, like every other emotion, it can be beneficial, or it can interfere with what we are trying to accomplish in life.

Coaching insights and summary

These six case studies demonstrate the process of emotions-centred coaching. This methodology does not exclude conversation and language nor does it omit the body. We are coherent, and our whole being is involved in the resolution of challenges. Emotions-Centred Coaching simply gives us a focus, an entry point, a place for the client to expand their awareness and understanding and a set of tools for the future. In those ways, it can be a powerful approach to coaching that produces sustained results.

If you desire to explore coaching in this manner, a good place to start is with your own emotional literacy. The first step in that process is a practice of noticing and naming the emotions you experience every moment of every day. There is no shortage of material to practise with. Writing down your emotion every few hours in a small notebook over a two or three week period will teach you a lot. You'll see the emotions you can name easily and those you struggle with; the ones that repeat often; the ones that are missing. You'll also notice that over that period you begin to name emotions you didn't at the beginning of the exercise. This is evidence of your growing emotional vocabulary. From there, deconstructing the emotions into their core story, the impulse you felt and how they serve you will take you deeper into understanding.

This is the journey I took to build my emotional competence, and it has transformed the way I understand myself and my coachees. It has made emotions supportive allies rather than an internal force I'm constantly battling. It has made emotions my friend rather than my adversary. I wish the same for you.

~

Connect with the Author

Thank you for sharing this time and exploration. I hope it has produced insights and connected with your work and life. To learn more about me, my work or ways to develop emotional literacy please visit my website www.schoolofemotions.world. You can reach me directly at dan@schoolofemotions.world

IV

THE IDENTITY

Covered in this section

As we continue our journey to the deeper levels of a person's psyche, we move to the level of identity. Identity, in psychological terms, is how you define yourself: who you are, the way you think about yourself, your personality, your beliefs and views of the world around you. Why is this important? Because at this level we are creating our values, self-worth, self-compassion and self-image, all of which are critical to overall well-being and mental health. This is why it is important for a coach to understand these and be able to support clients to remove limiting beliefs and ways of being, and replace them with more productive ones that generate resourceful behaviours, which in turn impact their values and sense of identity.

Chapter 8: Ways of Being: The Way to Be Who You Want to Be
David Ross
David shares with us a unique and powerful conversational change technique called 'Ways of Being' that can help a client not only to identify an unhelpful 'way of being' (and behaving), but also to understand its associated benefits and values and, most importantly, its consequences that interfere with the client achieving their goals. David shows us how to transform these habitual behavioural systems that naturally dominate

our unconscious experience into new, positive and resourceful Ways of Being.

Chapter 9: Values: Developing a Powerful Guidance System
David Ross
David explores and demonstrates ways in which values drive behaviours, motivation and decisions and shares techniques to realign and install values so that they generate changes in behaviour in line with our goals and outcomes. Values operate at the level of identity in terms of *who* we believe we are. They also operate in terms of *why* we do the behaviours we do. Working with your client's values in the contexts of work and relationships, for example, can fast track huge unconscious shifts in their behaviours and thus the results they achieve.

Chapter 10: Coaching for Identity Grows Purpose and Performance
Aidan Tod
Aidan introduces us to techniques to identify who we really are at our best. Using clues from our past and present and exploring the future with imagination, our clients can get in touch with who they are when they are at their very best and live lives congruent with their real identity. He shows us how we can take our clients out into their futures and link them to their true purpose and identity. They can then make confident and exciting choices about career direction and changes which align them with their most fulfilling professional lives.

CHAPTER 8

WAYS OF BEING

The Way to Be Who You Want to Be

David Ross

We each develop habitual Ways of Being, behavioural systems that create a way of thinking, feeling and acting that seem normal and real. Some of these serve us: others do not. By identifying and changing these, we can powerfully redefine ourselves.

Covered in this chapter
- How Ways of Being are formed at an early age
- Case studies to demonstrate the impact of Ways of Being
- Real examples of coaching Ways of Being with clients
- How to pre-frame to successfully set up a client session
- The 7 factors you need to know to uncover the structure of the problem
- How to create and install new Ways of Being that lead to choices for a client

---

INTRODUCTION

Human beings have been designed to be habit-forming right from the moment we are born. The challenge is that as children we don't make conscious logical choices about the habits we are forming. Instead, we have a naturally instinctive way of reacting to the circumstances and stimuli that surround us.

At the time we unconsciously make these choices they seem to serve us well as children. As we grow and develop through different experiences and want different outcomes, these old behavioural systems can become barriers to achieving our potential.

Ways of Being is a leading-edge conversational change technique. This highly powerful and effective conversation (created by David Ross) works across and through the matrix of millions of possible interceptions of thoughts, feelings and behaviours all triggered by memories, unconscious decisions, values, beliefs and strategies. The Ways of Being intervention signposts the journey to making alternative choices or adjustments to how we want to define ourselves.

This chapter reveals a clear demonstration of the 'Ways of Being' tool in practice and how to create a shift in an individual's behaviours. The reader is taken step by step through the technique and the methodology used and is given a clear understanding of the kinds of questions to be posed enabling the client to transition from an old unhelpful Way of Being to a new one.

What are Ways of Being?

The Ways of Being (WOB) tool is a model for a coaching conversation developed over many years of experimentation and client feedback.

The term 'Way of Being' is something that people naturally identify with, and can connect with, very quickly.

People are familiar with hearing expressions like 'John has a particular Way of Being around others that isn't particularly helpful' or 'Why are you being that way?'

How a person is 'being' at a particular moment in time is the result of a confluence of:

- Behaviours (internal or external)
- Skills that are activated unconsciously
- Values that drive the motivation to do the behaviours
- States*, for example awareness, curiosity, calmness, determination, anxiety
- Beliefs that underpin the WOB
- Emotions**, for example fear, anger, love, sadness.

These systems are fundamental to the way human beings function because they enable strategies for success to be actualised and easily repeated.

*States, such as curiosity, alertness, frustration, confusion, calmness and energised are more to do with the mind than the body.

**An emotion is defined as those feelings such as anger, fear, sadness, guilt, happiness, love. These are deep basic strong feelings derived from a mood, or from relationships with others, and held in the body as opposed to the mind.

The systematic approach outlined in the chapter will help you:

- Understand the relationship between early life experiences and behavioural patterns still being used today
- Discover the anatomy of Ways of Being and use that map to help create deep change
- Have conversations that are natural to the client and create deep change
- Develop confidence in the sequence of eliciting problems and helping a client generate solutions

- Know where a client is at each stage of the journey to changing a Way of Being.

How Ways of Being are formed

A key principle of Ways of Being is that human beings are designed to generate habits. Being habit-forming is positive for us in that it enables us to perform and repeat both physical and mental tasks without having to consciously think about how to do them. We go through a process of consciously learning to do something before the behaviour or skills become unconscious – like learning to drive.

Forming behavioural habits makes us very efficient in how we go about our day-to-day routines and activities. Ultimately, we spend most of our waking moments on autopilot. As we journey through life our brains encode and store our experiences and, as part of this process, our experiences become generalised in order to make our behavioural choices easier to make, quicker to execute and, ultimately, more efficient. These generalised sets of experiences form behavioural systems: 'Ways of Being.'

CASE STUDY 1: 'I AM GOING TO SURVIVE ON MY OWN'

Ways of Being are underpinned by the beliefs and emotions that sponsored their creation and are expressed in words that literally mean a person is *being* a certain way. For example the following string of thoughts and emotions created a Way of Being: 'I have been rejected' (belief), 'I am afraid of being hurt' (belief), 'I don't need anyone else' (belief). Sadness, anger and fear (emotions). 'I am a survivor' (belief). The Way of Being resulting from this string of thoughts was: 'I *am* going to survive on my own.'

In summary, the Way of Being 'I am going to survive on my own' has a number of component parts:

- **An experience.** My parents sent me to boarding-school aged five, where only Afrikaans was spoken (where an unconscious decision was made)
- **Beliefs.** 'I have been rejected'; 'I am afraid people will hurt me'; 'I'm not loveable'
- **Emotions.** Fear, anger, sadness and hurt
- **Values.** Resilience, independence
- **Skills.** Crisis management, control, creativity, strategies and tactics
- **Behaviours.** Thinking quickly, dissociation from others, not letting people get close, not trusting others, watching and listening for people's intentions
- **States.** Anxiety, anticipation, determination.

CASE STUDY 2: 'I AM SAFER BEING QUIET'

A six-year-old boy is sitting in class with a puzzled expression on his face trying to understand how to do a maths problem. The teacher comes up to him and asks what's wrong. The boy replies that he does not understand how to do the sum and the teacher replies, 'Well you are so bad at maths.' From that moment onwards, the boy becomes afraid of being humiliated in maths classes and this is compounded by his classmates who don't waste any time baiting him about his lack of ability at maths. The boy becomes an adolescent 15-year-old who sits in a maths class unable to speak or think clearly as he is afraid of being humiliated. The underlying belief is, 'I am bad at maths and people think I'm stupid.' The leader who held this belief, 'I'm stupid,' was leading a significant part of an international bank and would often respond very negatively to ideas on how to make improvements. The outcome was that he was perceived as a huge blocker to improvements, and as a result was invited to have some coaching. He made such huge changes in his Ways of Being that his part of the bank became one of the highest performing in their sector globally.

CASE STUDY 3: 'I AM A PEOPLE PLEASER'

A 7-year-old boy's parents have split up and his mother marries another man. Whenever the boy comes home from school his stepfather tries to find some fault with his schoolwork and then subsequently beats him.

The boy decides that for him to be safe he needs to 'please people.' He became a 'people pleaser.' Today the man is an HR director who is unable to give strong direction to his team, he can't say 'no' and instead of delegating to his people is constantly overwhelmed by all the things he has agreed to do.

CASE STUDY 4: 'I AM DIFFERENT'

A five-year-old child, whose middle-class parents ran a pub, lived in a working-class area in Manchester, and went to a school where his clothes and toys were very different to his peer group who were always pointing that out. He had more pocket money than his peers and his house was different. He began to feel different and then one day he got polio in his right leg and had to wear a calliper. This compounded his perception of being different. 'I am different' became a Way of Being. Because it was a Way of Being there became an over-focus on being different and he found himself isolated and unable to build relationships. When he became an adult, he worked as a successful architect but had difficulty managing the teams of people working for him. Being intensely very different is not helpful in building relationships. As a result of this propensity to be different he was always in disagreement with his colleagues and clients. His boss subsequently gave him three months to change.

CASE STUDY 5: 'I WISH I WAS A BOY'

A ten-year-old girl wants to have as good a relationship with her father as her elder brother has.

She decides to play football, go to football matches with them and do everything that boys do in an attempt to be like a boy. 'If I am like a boy then maybe my dad will love me as much as my brother.' She became so much like a boy in character, in style and in behaviour that when she eventually wanted a partner and to get married, she found it very difficult. She had lost a lot of her femininity, mentally and physically. She became very lonely and it was this loneliness that motivated her to seek change.

People will not give up on their Ways of Being unless they can understand and are motivated by the payoffs for doing so. 'How I am being has got me to where I am today' they might say. Your response to that might be: *Well that's right, your Way of Being has got you to where you are today, and the question is, how much further could you go if you changed it?*

Once a seemingly unhelpful Way of Being is discovered, the motivation to change is critical to support the client to become able to let it go. This can be achieved by using the contrast frame in the Ways of Being elicitation process to enable the client to contrast their Way of Being in relation to their behavioural change outcomes.

The Way of Being process in Figure 8.1 enables you to explore this in depth.

HOW TO ELICIT WAYS OF BEING

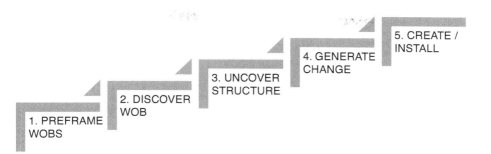

Figure 8.1: The Ways of Being process

The following are the sequence of steps that define the process for eliciting Ways of Being.

Note: The Ways of Being elicitation process that follows is illustrated with a real-life example. The questions used to elicit this Way of Being are examples of the kinds of questions required to help the client to identify their unhelpful Way of Being. The style of conversation is non-directive and uses embedded suggestions to direct the client's thoughts to where they will find the answers. The structure of each question is designed to guide the client through the maze of their unconscious to discover and understand what their Ways of Being are and how they generate their behaviours today.

1. Pre-frame Ways of Being (framing the process of Ways of Being for the client)

a. Start by telling a story about yours and / or someone else's Way of Being (WOB). Telling your own story is very powerful as it makes the client feel as though the coach is no different to them and importantly stimulates them to start thinking about their own WOB.

b. Explain how WOBs are formed and how a person makes conscious and unconscious decisions about their world and events they experienced which lead to choices about how they are going to respond to those events and decisions. Example one: 'If my parents don't love me, then no one else will either and it's best not to need people but to survive on my own.' Example two: 'My home is a dangerous place. My stepfather wants to hurt me; therefore, I need to make sure that I please him (and others) in order to avoid being hurt.'

c. Explain how a WOB is anchored deep in their unconscious mind by the beliefs and emotions that created it.

Without the emotions or the beliefs the WOB cannot exist. When these anchors fall away the WOB system dissolves and the behaviours that have been held within it, as defaults, now become choices. The person is able to choose to behave in whatever way is appropriate and is the most optimal choice of behaviour for the task at hand. This freedom enables the person to develop new behaviours without them being overridden by their WOB.

2. Discover Ways of Being

At the beginning of the elicitation process, tell the client you are going to summarise the key points on the flip chart. (A working example of this is shown later in this chapter.) Split the flip chart (or whiteboard) in two placing a large circle in the middle. Put the age on the top left-hand side (e.g. 0–7 years old). Place the behaviour or skill to be developed on the top right-hand side. Place the Way of Being in the middle circle.

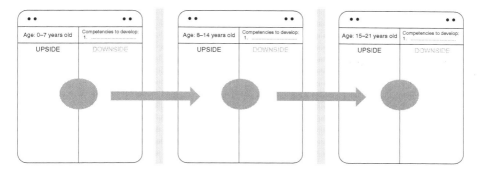

Figure 8.2: Flip chart format for output notes

Identifying a Way of Being

Coach: *First of all, we are going to have a conversation about your life between 0-7 years old followed by 8–14 years old and then 15–21 years old. As I ask you questions about those times and you start to tell the story, you may have the experience of Ways of Being expressions just dropping naturally into the conversation.*

So, let's talk about that 0–7-years-old period of your life. (If the client says 'I don't remember anything about that time,' say that it doesn't matter we can start on the 8–14-years-old period and then come back the 0–7-years-old period later.) OK, *so you were born in the Belgian Congo of missionary parents?*

Client: Yes, and I used to go hunting and fishing in the jungle with the Africans every day after doing schoolwork with my mother who was a teacher. I would do schoolwork between 7 am and 9 am. I really felt that life was a great adventure at this point and then one day out of the blue, my parents told me that they were sending me to a school 500 miles away. When I arrived at the school, I discovered that it was run by Afrikaners who did not speak any English or French.

Coach: *How old were you then?*

Client: I was six years old.

Coach: *So, what happened then?*

Client: Well, I was left with an English family at the mission station where I was to go to school. There were the two parents and two young children. One child was about 18 months and the other about three years old.

As my parents left me with the family I felt abandoned, rejected and terribly alone. I cried all night and when I got up in the morning for breakfast I felt very angry. I made my way to the breakfast table and sat down to eat. As I sat there eating I felt my feet being prodded under the table. I kicked out and broke the nose of the 18-month-old kid. There was blood everywhere.

The parents told me I couldn't stay with them and later that day I moved in with a family of 11 children who were Afrikaners. They did not speak any English.

Coach: *So how did you see the world at this point?*

Client: I believed that my parents and now others had rejected me and that I was not loved or wanted.

Coach: *How did you react to that observation?*

Client: I decided that I would need to be self-sufficient and to not need other people because they hurt me.

Coach: *So, what seems to best describe the Way of Being you decided on that day? What words best capture it?*

Client: I don't need anyone else; 'I am going to survive on my own.'

Coach: *I am going to place 'I am a going to survive on my own' in the middle circle now.*

Identifying the upsides and downsides

As the elicitation process progresses to the upside and downsides of the Way of Being, place the 'upside' on the top left-hand side of the flip chart and the 'downside' on the right-hand side.

When discovering the upside and downside, always start with the upside first. This helps the client to see benefits and strengths (positives) in their WOB rather than immediately feeling negative about the downside.

Place each of the outputs for the upside and downside in bubbles so that the client has a visual representation to reinforce their experience of the discovery process. The illustration is an example of the output from the Way of Being elicitation below. The summarised words chosen for each part of the conversation have been highlighted in the full answers given by the client shown in Table 8.1.

Coach: *Well done. That was good work. How do you feel about that Way of Being and do you recognise it living in you today?*

Client: It feels true to me and yes I recognise it as a fundamental Way of Being in me today.

Coach: *OK what we are going to do now is to create a contrast frame in which you will be able to evaluate your WOB in the context of the behaviour / skills you want to develop. At the beginning of the coaching process you agreed that the most important skill to develop to enable you to achieve your goals is to be able to build effective relationships. This will enable you to achieve / improve your career goals, your friendships and partner relationship. How do you know that is still true?*

Client: It's still true because I know more than ever that being able to sustain my relationship with my partner in life is the most important thing to me and right now I am endangering that relationship because of my Way of Being which is 'I am going to survive on my own.'

Also, in terms of my career I realise that people won't want to work for a manager who does not relate easily to them and who appears to think only of himself.

Coach: *Those are great learnings and realisations. Now, I am going to create a simple contrast frame on the flipchart and we will start talking through the upsides and the downsides of your WOB 'I am a survivor' in the context of building relationships.*

There will be upsides to this WOB that you may never have noticed consciously before. I want you to notice these and consider how to utilise them in the context of building relationships. You will naturally be more conscious of the downside and these are the behaviours that you will be able to stop doing automatically once the 'anchor' is reframed and the default falls away. I just want to remind you that all behaviour is appropriate in the right context.

Let's look at the upside of this Way of Being first. I want you to 'put on' your Way of Being 'I am going to survive on my own' as though you are doing it now, feeling what you feel, seeing what you see, hearing what you hear as you are being that way. Now from that perspective, what is the upside of this Way of Being in the context of building relationships? What is present in that Way of Being that supports building relationships?

Table 8.1: Table illustrating questions and answers defining the upside and downside of the Way of Being 'I am going to survive on my own.' The coaching outcome is to be able to build effective relationships.

Upside	Downside
(Step 1: suggested questions to use in brackets)	(Step 2: notice the chunking down here to raise motivation to change)
Coach: *(What is present in your Way of Being 'I am going to survive on my own' that supports building relationships?)* Client: Well I **observe people closely** in order to anticipate what they will do next, for example will they do something bad to hurt me in some way? Coach: *Very good. Observation is an important aspect of building relationships. There will be other things to learn about in terms of what to observe and how to utilise those observations effectively in relationship building during your coaching programme.* *When you are observing people, what do you notice about them?* Client: Their facial expressions, body language and voice.	Coach: *Let's look at the downside of this Way of Being and the original intent of observing people. What is the original intent of this WOB in the context of observing people?* Client: Its purpose is to look for negative signals and cues that let me know if the person is untrustworthy and likely to hurt me in some way. Coach: *What emotions are present to cause you to react that way?* Client: **I fear being hurt** and am anxiously waiting for it to happen. Coach: *What do you do to live with the fear of being hurt?* Client: I avoid getting close to people. Coach: *Now finally let's look at the original intent for remembering people's names. What is the original intent for that?*

Coach: *Those are very useful things to notice in a positive way as you build the relationship.*

Coach: *As you reflect on this Way of Being 'I am a survivor,' what else do you notice about how this WOB supports building relationships?*

Client: I notice being in a heightened **state of alertness ready to take action**. In fact, I have noticed that this seems to have a positive impact with those people who are action oriented and less well with those who are quieter and more thoughtful.

Coach: *Good. Now, what else do you notice about this Way of Being that supports building relationships?*

Client: I have a great memory for names.

Coach: *That's a great asset and very useful in building relationships. So now you can see that there are some useful resources present in this Way of Being that can be focused positively in building relationships. You will be able to utilise these when we construct a strategy for building relationships.*

NOW let's turn to the downside of this WOB in the context of building relationships.

Client: It's very similar to the state of alertness. It's about remembering the people that I suspect of wanting to hurt me so that I can avoid them.

Coach: *So, in summary, what are the downsides to this WOB?*

Client: **I don't trust people** and am wary of having a relationship. I tend to treat people as tasks rather than as the people they are. I feel myself **dissociating from them** and am unable to engage. I feel constantly tense and anxious around others.

Coach: *Well done. How did you find the process?*

Client: It was challenging and has given me insights into what I need to be able to change.

A more in-depth explanation of Active Listening and its role in coaching can be found in Chapter 3: 'The Transformational Impact of Active Listening' by Colin D. Smith. The Ways of Being elicitation depends upon strong listening skills. Listen, repeat back what you heard and keep exploring. Listen for the words that define Ways of Being and write down the client's words and descriptors.

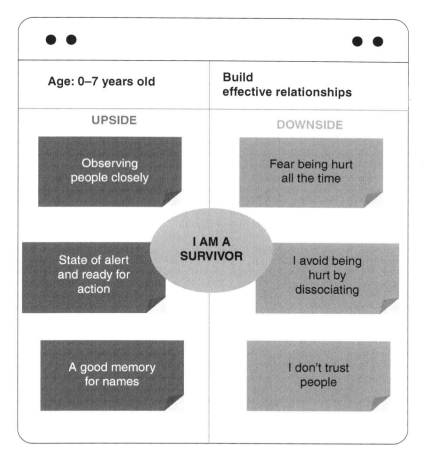

Figure 8.3: Flip-charted result of the Way of Being
'I am going to survive on my own'

Note: in order to be free to choose to build relationships there are a number of beliefs and emotions the client can learn to let go of.

To develop greater fluency with the language of emotions please read Chapter 7: 'Getting to the Heart of the Matter: Emotions-Centred Coaching' by Dan Newby.

This is the end of the elicitation process for Ways of Being. The follow-on, having completed the elicitation of the 0–7-years-old period, will be the 8–14 and 15–21-years-old periods *if* it's appropriate and necessary to do so. The decision to go further into the later periods will become obvious as the client's story unfolds. If the first WOB (0–7) is not the cause of the problem the client is looking to resolve, you may seek to uncover the second and third WOB. Once the coach is well-practised with the elicitation process, each period will take 30–45 minutes to complete.

3. Uncover structure

In order to be free to choose to build relationships we need to uncover the 7 component parts so we know what parts to change.

The 7 component parts of a WOB are one or more of the following:

- The originating belief underpinning the WOB
- Emotions underpinning the WOB
- Values that drive and motivate the client to display the WOB
- Other beliefs associated with the WOB
- States
- Skills specific to the WOB
- Behaviours specific to the WOB

The script for the elicitation of these components is as follows:

1. Decisions underpinning the WOB
Coach: *When you were between 0 and 7 years old and you created the WOB 'I am a survivor,' what had you decided about your world or yourself?*

Client: Well, I decided that my parents did not love me and that I wasn't loveable.

2. Emotions
Coach: *OK, so the decision underpinning this WOB is I'm not loveable and what are the emotions that were created by that decision.*

Client: Great anger, sadness and fear. (Explore further if appropriate).

3. Values associated with the WOB
Coach: *What was important to you about 'I am going to survive on my own?'*

Client: Independence became really important to me.

Coach: *What else besides 'independence' became important to you?*

Client: Anticipation of what others might say or do to hurt me. Anticipation became important.

Coach: *OK, so independence and anticipation were important then. Are they still important today?*

Client: Yes, they are. (Explore further if appropriate.)

4. Belief associated with this WOB

Coach: *What else did you believe other than I am not loveable?*

Client: I believed that no one else would love and look after me, so I had better do that for myself.

5. State associated with this WOB

Coach: *OK, now what state is necessary to do this WOB well? As you are aware of your WOB now, you can notice what state is present. What is that state like?*

Client: It's a sharpness of mind and awareness, an edgy feeling, like anxiety.

Coach: *So, it's a sharp edgy feeling like anxiety. Is it anxiety?*

Client: Yes, I think so.

6. Skills associated with the WOB

Coach: *Let's talk about the skills you developed in order to be able to do this WOB well. What are you really good at when doing this WOB?*

Client: I became good at survival skills like, **physical strength**, **verbal reasoning** and **creating strategies for getting what I want on my own**. (Explore further if appropriate.)

7. Behaviour associated with this WOB

Coach: *In terms of behaviours that you developed to do this WOB well, what were the key ones?*

Client: I can **dissociate (separate / distance)** myself from the fear I feel around others. I am always **observing** everything about others and what they are doing. (Explore further as appropriate.)

Summarise the set of 7 component parts:

Coach: *OK, so let's summarise that set of component parts.*

COMPONENT PARTS	
Decision ➡	'I am not loveable.'
Emotions ➡	Great sadness, anger and fear
Values ➡	Independence and Anticipation
Belief ➡	'No one else will love and look after me so I had better look after myself.'
State ➡	Sharp, on edge and having an anxious feeling
Skills ➡	Physical strength, verbal reasoning and creating strategies for getting what I want.
Behaviours ➡	Dissociation: (The ability to step back and view events or yourself from a distance such that there are no feelings experienced, just things as they are – dispassionately)
	Observation: (Watching, listening and intuiting about what people do and how they do it)

Figure 8.4: Component parts

4. Generate change

The overall intention now is to free the client from defaulting to their unhelpful Way of Being as this is hindering them moving forward and getting the results they want in their life. Remember that a WOB is held in place by the decisions and emotions that underpin it ('I'm not loveable,' sadness, anger and fear in the example above). When those decisions and emotions are reframed the default state disappears, and the client is able to develop new behaviours. The client is also able to *choose* to do those really useful behaviours that were embedded in the WOB, as opposed to defaulting to them.

It could also be important to reframe other beliefs associated with the WOB (as in the example above: 'No one else will look after me so I need to do that for myself').

Once these changes have been made, go back and associate the client into the old Way of Being. Have them notice how each feature of the upsides and downsides have changed. How does that leave them feeling and what do they need next?

Coaches can use their favourite interventions to bring about change to limiting beliefs and negative emotions that underpin the Way of Being. Some of these may be: Neuro-Linguistic Programming (NLP) interventions, timeline therapy, gestalt therapy and cognitive behavioural therapy.

5. Create / install new WOB

a) Creation process
One of the successful principles of human design is that habits generate efficiency. It therefore makes sense to create a new Way of Being for your client to enable them to actualise themselves towards their vision and goals through Ways of Being that are designed to deliver success behaviours in that context. New Ways of Being can be generalised to cover every aspect of a client's life.

In our example of 'I am going to survive on my own,' the client chose to create a new WOB 'I am going to live my life to the full.' You can check this out for yourself in terms of its viability to drive a successful life, by taking each of the following contexts of your life and asking yourself 'What will happen if I am living my life to the full in the context of ...':

- Work
- Family
- Relationships
- Health
- Personal development
- Spiritual growth.

To discover how to contextualise values in order to elicit them correctly, see Chapter 9: 'Values: Developing a Powerful Guidance System' by David Ross.

When at this stage of the client's coaching, take time to think about the optimal set of generalisations (e.g. I am living my life to the full) that are appropriate for the client and their outcomes. The statement needs to be action-oriented and a statement of intent. Once you have agreed the appropriate statement you will need to work through the design of the elements that are going to enable the new WOB.

One or more of the following are essential ingredients for the new recipe:

- Empowering beliefs
- Positive states
- Values
- Skills
- Behaviours.

Once you have agreed the key elements the next step is to resource each of those key elements. Help the client to create new beliefs and build new behaviours and skills if they don't already exist in their experience. Once you have agreed what is present already and what needs to be created, check that each element is still 'fit for purpose.'

Now you are ready to install the new Way of Being.

b) Three-step installation process
The method below uses a circle or space in which to 'stack' the positive resources and connect them all together to create a new 'system' that generates the new Way of Being. The 'stack' can be easily turned on / activated by simply stepping into the

circle that was originally created. The circle can be 'folded up' mentally and taken with the client wherever they go. Whenever they want to re-associate to the Way of Being, they simply lay down the circle and step into it again, fully associating with the Way of Being. For the purposes of demonstrating this process the WOB is 'I am living my life to the full.'

Step 1: Create a space in the middle of the room

- Invite your client to imagine a circle on the floor. Invite them to create a personal symbol or representation of the circle. (This could be a spotlight, a pool or anything else they think fits. It can be any colour, size or texture.) This is important to being able to continue to use the WOB long term and to integrate the WOB fully.
- Invite your client to place the new WOB 'I am living my life to the full' in the centre of the space.
- Ask the client to step into the space and fully immerse themselves into and associate with the WOB as though they were trying it on for size.[1]
- Say to them *Consider this new Way of Being 'I am living my life to the full.' What does it feel like, what are you seeing and what does it sound like?*

---

1   To associate means to connect fully with an idea, a feeling, a sound, a picture, or an event. Associating with a belief for example would mean the client imagining that they had stepped into a picture that represents the belief, seeing what they see, feeling what they feel and hearing what they hear. In this way the new concept or idea can be fully experienced and adjusted if necessary so that it fits in with the way that the client thinks. Using the circle or space method for anchoring the new beliefs, states, emotions etc. enables the client to take each component part of the new Way of Being and associate with each resource in turn in order to validate them. As that process continues with each component part, all of them become associated, connected and accessible.

- Ask your client to repeat the words of the new WOB (inside or out loud) as many times as it takes for them to feel that they have assumed the new WOB. *As you fully experience this new way of being, how are things different?*
- Give them time and space to respond.
- Invite the client to step out of the space leaving the WOB in that space.

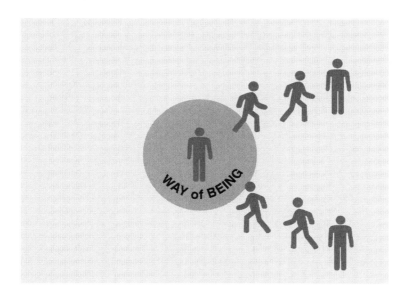

Figure 8.5: Way of Being: installation process

Step 2: Install each part of the new WOB in turn

- The next part of the process is designed to create each component part in the client's mind and to integrate each component within the new Way of Being such that all the ingredients become fully integrated with the WOB, thereby enabling it.
- All the components required to enable a Way of Being are:
  o One or more beliefs
  o One or more values

- One or more skills
- One or more behaviours
- One or more positive states.

Beliefs

Invite your client to identify the necessary beliefs for the Way of Being: *If you had one or two mission critical beliefs that supported this new Way of Being, what would they be?*

Two examples of beliefs enabling 'I am living my life to the full' are:

a. 'I have a vision, mission and well-formed goals for each area of my life that are relevant and congruent with who I am.'

b. 'I spend time developing and maintaining relationships that are fulfilling and to whom I add value.'

- Invite your client to:
  - Create a separate individual space in the room for the new belief separate from the WOB space
  - Step into the belief space and create their representation of that belief as a picture with feelings and sounds
  - (When the client is *fully* associated), step out of the belief space and take that belief with them and then step into the centre of the WOB space
  - Describe how this belief will enable the new WOB 'I am living my life to the full'
  - Notice how this belief reinforces the strength of the WOB.
- Be fully associated into the WOB space by repeating the words of the WOB. Then, repeat the words of the belief: 'I spend time developing and maintaining relationships that are fulfilling and to which I add value.'
- Notice how this belief connects to the Way of Being, how this strengthens and adds value to it and how they operate together and become co-dependent.

- Step out of the WOB space having left the belief and WOB integrated in that space.

Figure 8.6: Installing component parts of a Way of Being

(Repeat this process for each element of the new WOB, making sure that all elements are fully associated with each other and the WOB).

Step 3: Future pace the change[2]

Finally, suggest that the circle is a resource that the client can use anywhere.

---

2 Future pacing means to ask the client to imagine themselves in a future situation in which they are applying their new Way of Being. They notice how the Way of Being creates different results and how those results are optimal. *Think about a future situation that would have been challenging in the past. Now, as you are in that future event step into the circle and notice how things are different. How are they different?*

You can take this circle with you now. How are you choosing to take this circle with you now? You could fold it up and put it in your pocket. Whatever way you choose to keep it with you is fine. Now notice what happens when you choose to bring it back now. What happens?

Run through this cycle between three and seven times so that the client is totally comfortable being able to activate their circle whenever and wherever they want.

I know clients who still use their circle of excellence after 35 years. This client uses her circle for making big presentations to large groups of people. She knows that every time she uses it her results are both excellent and satisfying.

Coaching insights and summary

Ways of Being is a client-friendly intervention that achieves a lot of impact in a short space of time. It can be introduced into whatever coaching structure or practice that is being used.

Ways of Being provides the framework for generating a sustainable change and a series of building blocks for enabling the transformation for clients to be who they want to be in 5 steps:

1. Pre-framing Ways of Being
2. Discover Ways of Being
3. Uncover the structure
4. Generate change
5. Create and install new Way of Being.

Coaching in Action

Theory

We develop habitual patterns of thinking, feeling and acting that seem normal and run our lives. These can be changed through inquiry and reflection.

Action

Using case study one as a model, spend some time thinking through the early years of your life (periods 0-7 years old and 8-14 years). As you think about these periods, you can dwell on how you experienced your life and what you came to believe about yourself and the world around you. When you have settled on the beliefs and emotions, begin to wonder about how you decided to be as a result. Lastly, ask yourself if you notice that Way of Being actively driving you today. Having identified a Way of Being, think through all six aspects that power that Way of Being:

- A specific experience from childhood that carries positive emotion
- Behaviours (internal or external)
- Beliefs that underpin the WOB
- Emotions, for example, joy, love, anger or sadness. Also think about states, for example awareness, curiosity, calmness and determination
- Values that drive the motivation to do the behaviours
- Skills that are activated unconsciously.

Make a note of these and jot them down. Note how complete this feels to you. How well does it encapsulate the experience? Is there anything missing or that needs adding?

Now consider what new Way of Being will empower you to reach your full potential.

Design this new Way of Being following the process above. Using a contrast frame, so you can compare this new Way of Being with your present Way of Being. You can then start to plan the necessary changes that will enable the new Way of Being. This is an open invitation to reinvent yourself. You can start now!

~

Connect with the Author

Thank you for reading this chapter. Ways of Being is designed to enable deep transformational and sustainable change. Please feel free to get in touch if you would like further clarity on how to apply this in the context of your coaching, or just to answer any questions about the process itself. Please email me at: david. ross@cloud9apps.co.uk

CHAPTER 9

VALUES

Developing a Powerful Guidance System

David Ross

We are driven to make decisions and take action by an unconscious blueprint of values – a 'guidance system.' These drivers use emotions to signal what is right or wrong, good or bad and provide the criteria to help us make choices. Working with values provides a fast track way to identify blocks to success and a way to align a person's choices with their outcomes.

Covered in this chapter
- How values drive behaviour, motivation, and decisions
- Where values sit in the unconscious mind
- Aligning values to coaching goals and supportive behaviours
- A powerful four-step process to elicit, order, change and install values
- Case studies showing how coaching values generate changes in behaviour

---

INTRODUCTION

Values are dynamic drivers that motivate us into action. Light the touch paper and stand well back! They are powerful highly explosive personal emoting concepts that are at the very heart of what matters to us. Rather like volcanic energy, dynamite energy can be destructive if it is not harnessed appropriately!

Values are filters that sit between the conscious and unconscious. Through values, we can ascribe labels and meaning that enable us to know what is important and what to focus on. There are values that we are consciously aware of and values that we are completely unconscious of.

Every value has a set of criteria that let us know whether or not our value is being satisfied, for example, what is success and what is not success? These criteria will also provide the rationale for knowing what is right or wrong, good or bad.

Values provide us with a guidance system as we navigate life in pursuit of our ambitions, vision and goals. As we move towards our goals, values provide the energy and drive necessary to actualise ourselves through action.

Values have a specific function in relation to the behaviours, skills, emotions, beliefs and many other characteristics of the human mindset that have their individual functions too. They are important concepts that have impact when assisting a client to change. Values are fundamental drivers for behaviours and play a large role in behavioural change.

For further information on the creation of values read Chapter 8: 'Ways of Being: The Way to Be Who You Want to Be' by David Ross.

This chapter aims to provide an understanding of how values function, why they are important and the tools to generate behavioural change through them. You will learn how to discover values, troubleshoot behaviours using values, and hone values to sharpen the client's focus on what they want to achieve.

BENEFITS OF VALUES IN COACHING

- Values focus attention on what is important and what is not. This enables a client to distinguish between those tasks that are priority and those that are not. The higher the level of importance a value carries, the more a client will focus on activities and goals related to it
- Values enable congruency in the client's life because they signal what is right, what is wrong and what is good and bad. It is therefore key that values and associated behaviours are aligned with the client's vision and goals
- Values drive behaviours and enable fast tracking of behavioural change. A value is always consistently driving behaviours associated with it and this feature means that as long as newly developed behaviours are strongly associated with their corresponding values they will be actioned
- Identify where clients have developed an over-focus on values and don't have any vision or goals
- Neutralise a lack of direction and emotional swings
- Enable the client to become consistently positively motivated.

For great insights and to find out more about how to work with emotions read Chapter 6: 'The Heart of the Matter: A New Interpretation of Emotions' and Chapter 7: 'Getting to the Heart of the Matter: Emotions-Centred Coaching,' both by Dan Newby.

The systematic approach outlined in this chapter will help you:

- Utilise values to further a client's behavioural change in the context of their coaching programme
- Align values to support a client's goals with balance and focus

- Quickly locate and heal inner conflicts between values that create confusion, indecision and frustration
- Recognise how values hierarchies change across different contexts
- Root out the cause of any negative behaviour resulting from very specific values
- Connect new behaviours with the values that drive them.

HOW VALUES ARE STRUCTURED AND ORGANISED

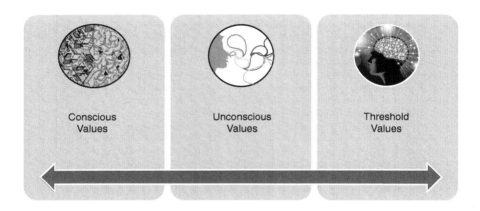

Figure 9.1: States of values consciousness

- Values we are *consciously* aware of are obvious to hear in the dialogue we are having with someone. When asked about their values the person will usually describe these first.

For more on the art of listening and honing your listening skills, read Chapter 3: 'The Transformational Impact of Active Listening' by Colin D. Smith.

- Values we are *unconscious* of will be less obvious in dialogue and need to be discovered through specific questions.
- *Threshold* values are *those* that lie in the deep unconscious and require different type of questions to uncover them.

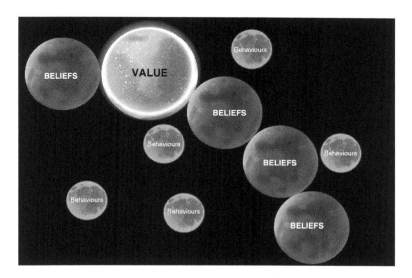

Figure 9.2: A Value System

Values lie at the centre of their galaxies with associated beliefs and behaviours orbiting around them.

These systems are generated through time and as William Massey suggests, within the age periods 0-7 years old, 8–14 years old, 15-21 years old and 21-28 years old.

See Chapter 8: 'Ways of Being: The Way to Be Who You Want to Be' by David Ross for more information.

Let's take a look at an example of the value of success and its associated beliefs and behaviours. Let's presuppose that success is number two in the values hierarchy in order of importance.

- Our unconscious minds hold values with kinaesthetic content that signals what is good or bad, right or wrong and confirms or denies action. In the context of success, the signal might be a feeling of elation that confirms 'success' or a feeling of disappointment that confirms 'not success'
- There will also be a visual component, for example a picture of a person standing on stage receiving an award
- There is also auditory content, for example listening to the sound of applause.

In this universe of success there are three beliefs. These are:

- 'I can be successful if I work hard'
- 'Success can only be created by setting clear goals for myself'
- 'I will be rewarded for success through recognition and money.'

The behaviours associated with success and the beliefs are:

- Working hard
- Strong focus on goals
- Learning how to get better / improving.

The way a value drives behaviour is like a detonator attached to a barrel of gunpowder. When the plunger on the detonator is pushed down, the resultant wave of strong energy fires off the behaviour associated with success.

Figure 9.3: Values detonate energy

As success is experienced through events confirming it, so the beliefs and behaviours become strongly reinforced through time. There will be more on how to identify the structure in the section on the elicitation of values.

Values are organised by context and hierarchy:

- Values exist across a wide range of contexts: family, health, relationships, personal development and spiritual development
- Values are organised hierarchically.

In the context of work / career the hierarchy of values might be as follows:

1. Fun
2. Results
3. Make a difference
4. Relationships
5. Financial security.

Within hierarchies, values are organised by order of preference similar to the way we organise our favourite songs in our MP3 player so that they can be selected preferentially.

In the hierarchy example above, *results* is at number two. This will have the impact of strong goal-oriented behaviour.

Also, this person is operating on the basis of *making a difference* at every opportunity in order to have the best chance of getting optimal results.

The *fun* factor adds a light-hearted approach and touch to what could otherwise be a very serious and tiring personal agenda.

The *relationship* element is an enabler to getting optimal results through cooperation with others and provides access to resources and options necessary to obtain results.

When operating this way, *financial security* will follow.

In this example fun (the most ambiguous value) is at the top of the hierarchy. The impact of this is to cause a generalisation of fun into each of the contexts of the other values.

- Having fun getting results as opposed to finding getting results arduous and wearing
- Having fun making a difference
- Having fun building and maintaining relationships
- Having fun creating financial security.

It's also possible to take each of the values and ask a question like *how could you make a difference in all your relationships; how could you help your relationships to move towards financial security?* This technique causes each value to become associated with other values in the hierarchy.

Value systems

Value systems are structured rather like a series of mini universes connected together.

The unconscious connects values through time and generates an interconnected system where values actualise each other and may even share common beliefs.

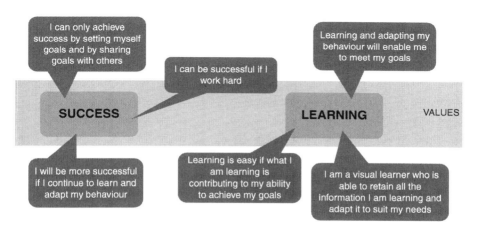

Figure 9.4: Values with shared beliefs

Generating change in values and values hierarchies

In order for something to become important a person will need to decide certain things. For example: if that person decided that life was dangerous then safety might become of paramount importance. If a person decides that relationships are hurtful, they might see independence as being important. If their experience is of being let down, then loyalty might become important (because people who are loyal don't let each other down).

Example of negatively framed values:

- Where the focus is on not failing because 'failure is bad,' then not failing becomes important.

These are positively framed values:

- 'When I sell more I can achieve success.'
- 'We can achieve our organisational goals through great relationships with our customers if we focus on treating them like one of the family.'

Step 1: Discovering the client's values

Discovering a person's values is the first step in the process of evaluating what values they experience as being important today.

The ingredients to elicit a value are the following:

What context is most relevant in making the change?
- Identify the context that is required to discover values in. This could be work, family, health, personal development, spiritual growth or relationships.

What specifically are the values in the context of work?
- Discovering what the values are will require a specific question like *What is important to you in the context of work?* Keep this question going until responses are exhausted. *'What else is important to you in the context of work other than Results?'*

Uncovering values held deep in the unconscious.
- Uncovering deeply held values means going fishing in the deep waters of the unconscious. (These values are called threshold values in NLP.) Uncovering deeply held values is done once the coach is not getting any new values other than those already elicited using the

question *What is important to you in the context of work other than value X?*

Process for eliciting deeply held values:

a. Ask the client to remember an event in which they were truly motivated at work.

I want you to remember an event in which you were truly motivated at work.

b. The next step is to make sure that they are fully associated into the event as though they were re-living the event again now.

Have the client step into the event and look through their own eyes, feeling what they felt, seeing what they saw, hearing what they heard as though they were there now.

I want you to remember that time as though you were there now looking through your own eyes, seeing what you saw then, hearing what you heard then and feeling what you felt then.

As they are now fully associated find out if they can feel a feeling of motivation there.

Now as you experience the event as though you were there, do you notice a feeling of motivation?

c. Assuming the answer is 'yes', ask the client imagine the memory as if it is a film: Get them to wind it backwards until they feel a feeling directly before the feeling of motivation starts.

(Winding the film backwards slowly enables the client to sense the point at which other emotions were felt and to be able to label those emotions. It is often the case that the emotion felt before the feeling of motivation is a deeply held value. The client will know whether it is or not once they bring it into consciousness.)

I want you to wind the film backwards until you are at the feeling just before the feeling of motivation and tell me the name of that feeling.

The client may say a number of words describing the feeling. These could be words like curiosity, anxiety, anticipation or challenge. Once they have voiced the word check it out as a value by asking them if that word 'X' is important to them.

Add the new value to the values list as appropriate.

A final check to see if there are any other undiscovered values: restate each value in the values hierarchy and then ask: *If all these values are being satisfied, what would have to happen to cause you to leave work?*

Let's look at the whole process of values elicitation in a practice example of a client who is sales director of a software company:

Coach: *What context of values would you like to work on?* (Work, relationships, family, health, personal development and spiritual growth.)

Client: I'd like to start in the context of work.

Coach: *What is it about work that you feel is important to work on in your values?*

Client: I want to have better relationships than I do at present, particularly with peers and stakeholders.

Coach: *What is important to you about work, what gets you up out of bed in the morning wanting to go to work?*

Client: Challenge is important to me.

Coach: *OK, so challenge is important to you; I'll just write that up on the flip chart. If challenge is important to you, what else is important to you about work other than challenge?*

Client: Results are important to me, getting results. (Coach writes up 'results' underneath 'challenge' on the flipchart.)

Coach: *OK, so results are important to you. What else is important to you in the context of work other than results?*

Client: Well I think relationships are important to me because without them it's not easy to get the results I want.

Coach: *If relationships, results and challenge are all important to you then what else is important to you in the context of work other than those values?*

Client: Respect is important to me. I want others to respect what I do.

Coach: *What else is important to you other than respect, relationships, results and challenge?*

Client: Ummmm! Let me think, I am finding it hard to come up with anything else!

Coach: *Let's look at going deeper into your unconscious to find any other values that are lying just outside your conscious grasp. I want you to remember a time at work when you were very motivated. As you remember that time I want you to be in the event as though you were there now, looking through your own eyes, hearing what you heard and feeling that feeling of motivation. Do you feel that feeling of motivation? OK. Good. Now wind back the film that you are in until you find the feeling just before the feeling of motivation. Now what is that feeling called?*

Client: That feeling is called Fun. (Threshold value)

Coach: *OK is fun important to you at work?*

Client: Yes, fun is important otherwise things get really wearing.

Coach: *I want you to think of another event at work that you found really motivating. OK you have one now? As you relive that event seeing what you saw, hearing what you heard and feeling what you felt, do you notice that feeling of motivation? Good now wind back the film until you notice the feeling before the feeling of motivation and what is that feeling called?*

Client: That feeling is a feeling of anticipation.

Coach: *Is anticipation important to you?*

Client: Yes, it is very important.

Coach: *Now let's do a final check to see if there are any 'threshold values.'*

If you had challenge, results, relationships, respect, fun and anticipation at work, what would have to happen to cause you to leave?

Client: I would leave if my boss had shown a lack of integrity over something that I told him in confidence.

Coach: *So is integrity important to you?*

Client: Yes, very important.

Coach: *So, let's look at the whole set of values now and discuss each one in turn to see what criteria you use to establish whether or not your values are being satisfied. For example, how do you know that a task, goal or project is going to be sufficiently challenging for you?*

The coach goes through each value in turn to get to fully understand the criteria for the value together with the behaviour the value is driving. The purpose of this is to be able to utilise the criteria when coaching a change in the focus of a value and to know which values will best drive new behaviours.

Step 2: Discover the present order and sequence of the values

In this example we now know what the client's values are in the context of work. What we don't know is the order and sequence of those values. That is, what is the hierarchical order of importance.

For what purpose do we want to know that? So that we can determine if the correct values are getting priority focus for the results the client wants. The following process will enable the discovery of the current hierarchy.

The list below is the order and sequence in which the client vocalised their values:

- Challenge
- Results
- Relationships
- Respect
- Fun
- Anticipation
- Integrity.

In order to discover the present order of importance of each value, ask the question *Today and right now which of these values is no. 1, which is no. 2,* and so on.

Let's presuppose the sequence of importance is:

1. Integrity
2. Results
3. Challenge
4. Respect
5. Anticipation
6. Relationships
7. Fun.

As you read this example ask yourself, *'What is it about this order and sequence of values that is likely to create issues for the client in this kind of role?'*

Step 3: Changing the order of values

The order of the values influences how those values play out in a person's life. In the example above the client's role means they need to focus on relationships with stakeholders and staff. The issue he has is that because integrity is the number one focus, his approach to their stakeholders is very matter of fact, black and white, right or wrong. This comes over as very judgemental and immediately puts people's backs up. Integrity *is* important and will be more effective further down the hierarchy.

Relationships are more important than integrity in the hierarchy and can be moved higher up in the hierarchy. Once this change in relative positioning has been made the client can be coached on a process for how to build effective relationships. The logic for the change in hierarchy is now in place and it is time to make the change in the hierarchical order of the values.

Using the following principles of:

a. The most ambiguous or vague value goes at the top

b. The relative changes in position are made to those values that are causing the issue.

Changes to the hierarchy might be as follows:

- 1 becomes Anticipation: this is the most ambiguous value and will help the client to look forward to getting results through relationships
- 2 becomes Fun: the finance world can be overloaded with seriousness so the fun aspect adds a little more light-heartedness into the client's approach
- 3 becomes Results: results are a key outcome in the interactions with stakeholders, they are going to be influenced to change the way they do things in order to improve overall results
- 4 becomes Relationships: effective relationships need to be established with stakeholders in order to support improved results. Without stakeholders onside this will be difficult to achieve
- 5 becomes Challenge: challenge will be required to create change in stakeholders' behaviour. This needs to be achieved with respect and through influencing skills
- 6 becomes Respect: respect is essential in terms of respecting the stakeholders' issues, problems and views in the context of how they operate now. This will bring stakeholders on side and enable them to become open to persuasion to change
- 7 becomes Integrity: integrity of data, systems, results is always going to be important in any business. This is more likely to be achieved by working hand in hand with the stakeholders rather than going head to head.

Figure 9.5: Installing values in a values 'highway'

Once the order of importance has been agreed with the client, it's time to install the values.

The process of making the mental change is about using imagination to construct the new context for the values to sit in. A values 'highway' can be created as a picture with feeling and / or sound content (whatever way suits the client's personal preference). For the purposes of this exercise let's imagine the highway is just that, a road stretching out into the distance.

You are going to ask the client to bring to mind a picture that represents value number one and to install the picture in the number one position on the highway. Go through each value in turn and ask the client to repeat the process for each value.

At the end of the creative exercise ask the client to check the whole highway of values to ensure that it feels congruent and that each value is sitting in its rightful position.

Now agree a series of tasks that the client will do every day to practise and to check that they are living through their values hierarchy.

Emphasise that values are bi-directional in focus. This means that they need to be looking through the values lens in both directions (at others as well as back at self).

Step 4: Installing a new value

Installing a new value is often necessary where the client does not have the relevant value(s) to act as appropriate guidance towards their vision and mission. This is often the case when creating vision and mission for either organisations or individuals. The missing value(s) can be identified during the vision / mission elicitation process by simply asking the question, 'So in the context of your vision X and mission Y, what needs to become important to you in order to maximise your focus?'

In order to install a new value have the client create a picture representing the value together with the feeling associated with it, and also any sounds or dialogue in the picture. Enhance the picture by directing the client to make it brighter, more colourful, more intense, and 3D as opposed to 2D. Suggest enhancements to the picture, feelings and sounds that will cause the value to become intensely motivating. Remember that the value will need to have the power (dynamite) to drive behaviours that will actualise the value. It's therefore very important to ensure that the value has a high level of positive energy associated with it.

Now the value is ready to install in its relative position in the values 'highway.' Go ahead and install it using the process outlined above this section.

CASE STUDY 1: UTILISING VALUES TO GENERATE CHANGE IN BEHAVIOUR AND OUTLOOK

An HR Director for a utilities company was experiencing huge swings in emotion. The problem with this was that he was reacting to situations, people or events in an uncontrolled, often negative way. Find out how to help your client to even out emotional swings and get back in control of their emotions.

For great insights and to find out more about how to work with emotions read Chapter 6: 'The Heart of the Matter: A New Interpretation of Emotions' and Chapter 7: 'Getting to the Heart of the Matter: Emotions-Centred Coaching' both by Dan Newby.

In this case, the person lived his life exclusively through his values and had never considered goals or outcomes. There were limiting beliefs compounding the lack of goals, for example:

- 'It is not OK to have what I want.'
- 'I will never have what I want because I always fail, so what's the point in thinking about it.'
- 'It's selfish to have what you want and it's bad to be selfish.'

Here is a sequence of interventions that enabled the client to even out emotional highs and lows and generate direction in his life.

1. The client learned how to formulate goals. Limiting beliefs about setting goals were reframed and let go

of. He was introduced to a model for creating vision, mission and goals across each context of his life.

2. Each value in the hierarchy was checked out for negative emotion content using the 'deeply held value elicitation process.' This enabled discovery of any negative emotions affecting specific values. Metaphorically, negative emotions in a value are similar to having water inside the detonator barrel discussed earlier in the chapter. The water will prevent the electric charge passing through to the gunpowder barrel that then fires off the energy to activate the behaviours. For example, 'fear of being open with others' may be present in the value of relationships.

This or any other negative content in the value can be removed / reframed.

DEVELOPING NEW BEHAVIOURS

CASE STUDY 2: OVER-FOCUS ON A PARTICULAR VALUE AND ANCHORING OF NEW BEHAVIOURS

A senior banker whose job was to manage the operations of the bank across a global network, wanted to build a more effective governance system. To implement this, he had to work in collaboration with each of the banks' country CEOs. He had to persuade and influence the CEOs to adopt new practices and integrate them into their organisation's ways of working.

In this example, the senior banker has a values hierarchy like this:

1. Integrity
2. Results
3. Financial success
4. Recognition.

From the values hierarchy you can see that his focus was on Integrity. He judged people by his own standards and was negatively hypercritical. Note that the value of 'Relationship' was not present in his values hierarchy. With this combination of values his relationships with the CEO group were not productive and he had difficulty driving change.

He agreed that he needed to change the importance of his values and reorder them and to learn a strategy for building effective relationships.

The following is the series of interventions used to enable the change in behaviour:

1. The client was enabled to recognise the need for effective stakeholder relationships through reframing.

2. A verbal reframe was used to install the value of Relationships and to alter the relative position of Integrity in the hierarchy. The reframe uses three out of four of the current values. *How much* integrity *are you having with yourself not to have* recognised *the importance of* relationships *in achieving* results? Once the client had processed the question he noticed a re-ordering taking place as a picture in his mind:

1. Results

2. Relationships

3. Integrity

4. Recognition.

As the client processed the question he created his picture of the value of relationships and changed the order and sequence of the values in the 'highway.'

3. Now that the client had the most effective values hierarchy for achieving what he needed to he learned how to build relationships through, rapport building techniques, honouring values, adapting his language patterns to match those of his stakeholders and creating win / wins

4. The client also learned how to influence a change in hearts and minds through the art of asking powerful questions

5. The new behaviours were anchored to the value of relationships through verbal repetition.

Within four months the client had started to turn things around and he began to get traction with the changes in governance he was seeking.

CASE STUDY 3: PRIORITISING AND RANKING VALUES

A director of human resources for a large food and beverage company had trouble leading her team. She was unable to say no to people and she did not feel able to tell her team members what she wanted them to do. Her annual review was disappointing as a result of her not having been able to deliver the results the board wanted from her.

Her relationship strategy had one type of boundary. Her single boundary in her relationship strategy was that everyone was a friend. In addition to the single boundary condition, her Relationship value was at number one in her values hierarchy and as a consequence she had over 300 friends whom she was constantly bumping into and chatting to every minute of the day. There were no Results, Success or Achievement values present in her hierarchy.

The solution was as follows:

- Remove limiting beliefs around having and achieving goals
- Install 'results' near the top of the hierarchy
- Coach her in how to set goals for herself and others
- Build a relationship strategy that prioritised her relationships in relation to her goals and the goals of her team.

Following these changes she was able to achieve the results that her board wanted from her and her team.

CASE STUDY 4: OVER-FOCUSING ON PARTICULAR VALUES

A global equities group in an investment bank was not performing and meeting profit targets.

The values hierarchy featured the following top two values:

1. Relationships
2. Results.

The consequence of this was that the equities teams put their client *relationships* above *results* for the bank. Clients were getting deal structures that favoured their clients more than the bank and this was affecting profits.

The whole group undertook team values sessions in which the values were realigned with Results at the top. The adjustment enabled the group to take a balanced view regarding client deals in which both the client and the bank profited in a win / win.

Coaching insights and summary

Values provide a very personal experience of coaching that makes it easy for the client to adapt and actualise change. Being consistently positively motivated increases the overall sense of well-being and being effective in life. Immediate results are achievable because behaviour is driven from the moment the connection between a value and the new behaviour is made.

Working with values within teams and organisations is a powerful way to achieve:

- Alignment and energise collective action towards mutual goals. Knowing how to recognise and utilise other people's values takes relationships with clients and others to a different level
- Understanding of the values of your team, business, partner or client which is one of the most important elements of being able to build and sustain a relationship through time.

Coaching in action

Theory

Values are drivers of motivation and behaviour and are key to creating inner alignment with goals and vision.

Action

- Start by noticing words occurring in the conversation that indicate a value(s).
- Be curious and ask what's important about that value.
- When discussing the goal for coaching, ask what is important about that goal. This will uncover values right at the start.
- Once you have established some values, start to drop those words into the conversation. Notice the change in the client's energy, physiology, breathing and voice.
- Note down your observations and explore these during the coaching process.
- Begin to wonder how you could utilise the client's values to fast track the change they are seeking.

~

Connect with the Author

Working with values enables fast and sustainable behaviour change. Enjoy the positive and powerful impact of working with values and thanks for reading this chapter! If you have any questions or feedback arising from the chapter it would be great to hear from you. Please email me: david.ross@cloud9apps.co.uk

CHAPTER 10

COACHING FOR IDENTITY GROWS PURPOSE AND PERFORMANCE

Aidan Tod

As coaches and leaders, we often come across people whose sense of identity comes from what they do, rather than who they are. Through supporting them to understand and appreciate more deeply who they really are at a deeper level, we enable them to make better choices about what they do that increases their performance, as well as their satisfaction and happiness in work and life.

Covered in this chapter
- A process for coaching identity
- Using past, present and future to discover identity
- How to use coaching tools like metaphor, anchoring, amplifying, affirming, championing, celebrating and witnessing to deepen awareness of identity
- How to use a Higher Power and Heroes to affirm identity
- What to do if your client gets stuck
- The power of resonant experiences to transform identity
- Suggested questions to use in this practice

INTRODUCTION

As coaches and leaders, we will often have come across individuals whose sense of identity comes primarily from their job role and career. What they do, rather than who they are, defines them. If you ask them 'Who are you?' they frequently answer with their job title and profession. Their self-worth is often tied up with their current job performance and goes up and down with the ebb and flow of their work life and achievements therein.

The idea of intrinsic self-worth as an incredible human being, whose value is priceless, has sadly often been forgotten. The boundary between self and job role eroded. Their incalculable value as a unique individual, partner, friend, mother, father, daughter, son, citizen is often ignored and their worth reduced to their economic value and contribution.

THE VALUE OF COACHING FOR IDENTITY

Through coaching for identity, we can help someone to uncover who they are and give them a language to share that with others, doing them a great service, enabling increased self-confidence, self-awareness and self-respect.

Knowing who they really are always increases their performance and effectiveness in the workplace and allows our clients to make informed choices about their current and future roles with greater confidence and sense of purpose.

So, coaching for identity has the potential to separate 'doing' from 'being' and help the client fundamentally understand who they are and *then* what they do at their very best.

It is rare for executives to ask directly, or seek coaching specifically, for issues of identity. Most commonly, it emerges as an issue within more typical executive coaching topics such as: developing their leadership, managing change, navigating career transitions and making choices about future career direction. This last area is where the issue of identity most commonly arises as people seek to align their work with their most important preferences and values.

A PROCESS FOR COACHING IDENTITY

Let us take the case study of an executive looking to make choices about future job roles and looking to get the most satisfying and developmental role.

In Western and some other cultures, people are raised from childhood to answer the question 'What do you want to be when you grow up?,' but experience teaches us that a far more important question that needs to be answered first is 'Who am I'? It is only when we can describe our strengths, skills, values, personality type, passions, ambitions, values and dreams that we can *then* confidently answer the question, 'What do I want to be when I grow up?' (and with our own voice, not that of a parent or boss).

So here are some of the approaches and tools we can use in coaching for identity in support of, in this case study, a clear future career direction. The client case study I will use as illustration in this chapter involved a senior executive in the financial sector – a regional manager – who was becoming increasingly dissatisfied with his role and who had a recurring thought that he should be working outside an office in the countryside, but was doing something completely different. As is often the case, my client suppressed these feelings for a long time. Conversations with himself became: But how would I pay the mortgage? It's a crazy idea! And what would I do anyway? I have no idea and no way of finding out? Et cetera.

Past, present and future: three ways to discover identity

In seeking to coach this client to discover more of who they are, (and therefore where they will be most fulfilled and contribute the most in their future career), we can look at their past, present and future in the different ways. While I follow the typical past, present and future order while describing this approach, the coach should follow the energy of the client and start with whichever time frame is most interesting to the client, and then keep following their energy to see where to go next. Simply ask the client, *In this process we will look at your past, present and future to discover clues about where you will be most fulfilled in your future career, where you will find you are working in line with who you feel you are at heart. Where would be most interesting for you to start? Past, present or future?* Pedagogically I ask what is most interesting as this relaxes the client and allows them to follow their interest. Asking which is most important to you, for example, can trigger a subconscious need to be right and try and please the coach.

Resonant experiences

As we examine past, present and future, we are exploring positive resonant experiences. A resonant experience is one full of positive emotions, actions and thoughts where the client resonates – like a tuning fork – with 'positive vibrations': a peak experience, in other words. It is where they feel happy, really alive and at their best doing something that feels like them being true to themselves and using many if not all their skills and attributes as a person. It may be a challenging situation but one where they feel up to the challenge and able to master it. Such experiences are clear signs of a person's true identity and vocation – what they feel they were born to do, their purpose. Helping the client unpack these moments in the ways described below enables them to understand why so much in their work-lives feels satisfying (or unsatisfying) and where they feel genuine or inauthentic in what they are doing and how they are being. The information revealed by them gives clear signposts for future career direction and satisfaction.

- In looking to the past, we are looking to discover who they were when they were most alive and having a positive resonant experience
- In the present, we are looking to discover who are they now, what energises them and who they are becoming
- With the future, we are taking the client there, and examining what is different about them there – who have they become? Who do they want to be, to be comfortable and fulfilled there?

Figure 10.1: Past, present and future: clues to identity

1. COACHING THE PAST

In looking to the past, we ask the client to look for peak experiences in their previous career, those moments when they felt most alive and satisfied. We ask them to think of a specific experience and take them back into it so that they can re-experience their thoughts and emotions. We're looking for the *most resonant* part of that resonant experience. So we will ask questions such as:

- Where are you?
- Who are you with?
- What is happening?

- What are you doing?
- What is the best part of this experience for you?
- How are you feeling there?
- What makes this such a good experience for you?
- Who are you in this moment?
- What does this reveal about who you are at your best?

We are unpacking all that this experience has to offer the client in the most resonant part of the whole experience. What we are looking for is the peak resonance within the resonant moment.

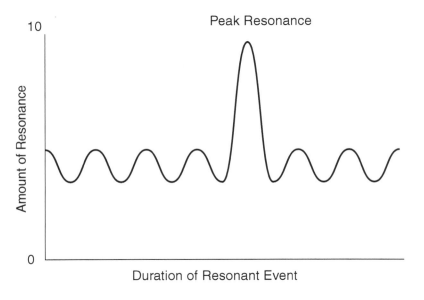

Figure 10.2: Resonant event: peak resonance

When looking to the past with the financial executive, we discovered through investigation that he had had a previous career in an emergency service. What resonated with him most in that previous career was responding in the moment to critical and life-threatening situations. Specifically, what resonated with him most was a large scale critical incident response simulation he had been involved in along with other services. This had been a peak experience for him and what would have been very threatening for most people was where he felt most alive and fulfilled using all his talents. We explored what was the most resonant moment of that event, and for him it was the most threatening part of the simulation when the greatest number of lives were at risk. His skill in preventing injury to others at that moment in the whole resonant event was the peak of resonance for him. We noted this and went on with his coaching using the methods and process in this chapter.

Metaphor

We can also go deeper into this resonant experience and discover what it reveals about their true identity by using metaphor, the language of the subconscious. So we might ask:

- *Which character from a favourite movie or story are you in this most resonant moment?*
- *And why that character? What qualities do you share with this character in this moment?*
- *Which qualities do you most value?*
- *What does that say about who you are?*

The use of metaphor typically deepens and anchors the client's understanding and retention of the important information in this experience and who they are at their best.

A more in-depth explanation of metaphors and their role in coaching can be found in Chapter 5: 'Coaching the Unconscious Mind through Metaphor' by Richard Haggerty.

Anchoring and amplifying

God / Creator / Higher Power and Heroes

To help create a powerful transformational moment of lasting value and great impact we can go even deeper into the identity of our client at their best by getting a powerful third-party insight into who they are at their best moments. Depending on our client's world view we use the appropriate most powerful third party, such as God or a Higher Power, a positive role model, a Hero or someone they look up to: for example Nelson Mandela. The subconscious, or heart of your client, will speak additional new positive affirming statements that reveal new additional aspects of their identity in the moment, and / or confirm and cement the positive attributes that the individual sees in themselves. You need only think for a moment of the encouragement you get when someone you respect affirms a positive trait in you, and your resulting determination to do more of the same or continue with that path, to see the even greater power in hearing from those you respect the most.

Someone you admire or respect

To discover whose input your client will benefit from most, we can ask:

- *Who do you most admire or respect – dead or alive?*
- *What do you feel your Hero sees in you in this moment?*
- *What do you hear them saying to you?*
- *How does that make you feel?*
- *What do you now know about your own qualities and character?*
- *How are they encouraging you to grow?*
- *Who do they say you are?*
- *What does this experience teach you about where you want to take your career?*

A Higher Power

Depending on our client's choice and beliefs, a client could choose God / Creator / Higher Power to replace the Hero role. With God / Creator / Higher Power, our client may believe that God is present and can speak to them in the moment. Our question structures change slightly therefore and become:

- *What does this Higher Power, however you conceive it, see in you in this moment?*
- *How is this Higher Power encouraging you to grow?*
- *Who does this Higher Power see you becoming?*
- *Who does this Higher Power say you are?*
- *What else do you hear this Higher Power say?*
- *How does that make you feel?*
- *What do you now know about your own qualities and character?*
- *What does this experience teach you about where you want to take your career?*

We have invited our client back to the most resonant moment in their past peak experience and invited them to imagine what the Higher Power or Hero said to encourage them, or how they saw them in that moment.

Such an exercise can truly help people to understand who they are at their best, to acknowledge and discover what is most important to them in their work and life, and to increase their desire to go further in their journey to discover their ideal next role / purpose, as they are discovering what truly motivates and energises them.

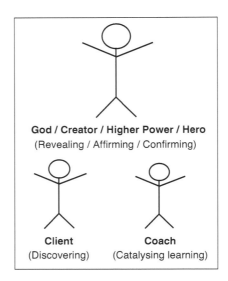

God / Creator / Higher Power / Hero
(Revealing / Affirming / Confirming)

Client
(Discovering)

Coach
(Catalysing learning)

Figure 10.3: Coaching with the Higher Power

Coaching posture and tools for coaching identity

Throughout sessions where we are coaching for identity, there are various attitudes and actions which we, as coaches, should be displaying and acting on when we observe the opportunity. Our attitude will be one of unconditional positive regard for the client, and in addition we can affirm, celebrate, champion, and witness our client's best self-identity when it appears and support them to notice the positives in themselves. As coaches, we can therefore play an important role in highlighting and anchoring the positive in our client's identity by doing the following:

Affirmation
Affirming the best when we see it:

- *What a brave thing to do. I see how courageous you are at your best.*

Share authentically with them how you see and experience them:

- *I see your resilience in that situation. That is a great attribute of yours, isn't it?*

Another technique that we can use to affirm and strengthen the client's identity is to get them to say aloud that positive aspect of themselves they've become aware of. Inviting a client to stand and state 'I am a leader who can inspire others' or 'I have all I need for my next role' can help them to take ownership of that aspect of themselves. Such ownership of course encourages the client to move to action with their heightened awareness of self.

Celebrating achievement
Clients often fail to acknowledge their achievements. It is important not to allow them to 'skip over' achievements but to invite them to celebrate the achievement with you, and then explore what that achievement says about who they are at their best and what it reveals about their identity.

Championing
We can all have moments of self-doubt or limiting beliefs about ourselves and of course our clients do too. As coaches we supportively challenge their self-doubt, pointing out the incongruities between how they feel and view themselves vs. how others view them and feel about them. We can coach at a deeper level to discover the root cause of their limiting belief, and then coach them into the truth about themselves and their true identity. This can be very powerful and liberating for our clients. I remember coaching one executive who had a strong desire to be creative, but he had agreed with some authority figure earlier in his life that he was not creative. When the strengths-

based psychometric we were using suggested that in fact he had a creativity strength, he was delighted. We explored the suggestion further and found the psychometric to be accurate. He went off to develop skills and knowledge around using his creativity so that he could apply it in the workplace.

Witnessing
The quality of attention we give to our client, our ability to remember pertinent facts about their identity from earlier coaching sessions perhaps, as well as our ability to highlight what we see happening in the moment, allows us to witness and highlight their best self or limiting beliefs and coach appropriately. Our honouring them, by our focused attention, witnesses itself to their worth.

A more in-depth explanation of Active Listening and focused attention and its role in coaching can be found in Chapter 3: 'The Transformational Impact of Active Listening' by Colin D. Smith.

---

2. COACHING THE PRESENT

We can and should use a similar approach to coach clients in the present. Who are they today? When coaching clients about the present it can be useful to ask them:

- *How would you describe your personality today?*
- *Your interests, motivations and passions?*
- *Your abilities?*
- *Your character?*
- *What does this tell you about who you are?*
- *What characteristics do you see developing?*
- *When you are most deeply fulfilled at work who are you being then?*
- *So, who are you today?*

Then we can coach the client's current identity in similar ways that we used for the resonant past to reveal more of who they truly are, apart from their job role.

Here is the process:

a. Take them to a current resonant experience. In the case study with the financial executive I am using, I took him to a recent resonant event and he chose another critical incident simulation he had been put in charge of, this time within the financial sector. This review of the present confirmed that he was still interested in crisis management – and this was still resonant for him. Recurring themes like this are real indicators of who someone is at their best and what work they will find most fulfilling and which aligns best with their deepest values.

b. Focus them in on the most resonant moment in that experience. Again, when doing just this with our financial executive, we found the higher the risk and the greater the stress in the crisis simulation for others, the more assured he became.

c. What do they notice about themselves in that place? The case study financial executive found that he had resilience, decisiveness and big picture strengths which enabled him to maintain clarity of thought and action while under great pressure in an increasingly complex scenario. He also discovered that this enhanced his leadership skills which were increasingly and happily relied on by others less confident under stress in the simulation.

d. Engage with the Higher Power or Hero. What are they saying to you today about your true identity? How are they encouraging you to grow? Who do they see you becoming? In my case study of the financial executive with an itch to work outside, my client chose an older man as Hero – someone who had worked in the same emergency service as he had done – and who, while now retired, did a lot of beneficial voluntary work for the local community. When engaging the Hero using the questions previously mentioned my client had his own courage, steady nerve, initiative and common sense affirmed by the Hero.

e. Unpack all that is happening in the current resonant experience. What does this reveal about their values, interests, passions, qualities, skills and strengths. Using this process we also discovered that, the client shared a passion to get back to a type of work that directly benefited people in need, that he preferred to work in teams of peers and preferred a series of projects to work on rather than a single large scale project which would take years to deliver. He liked working internationally, and so was not limited to the country where he was currently living.

f. Ask the client to think of a metaphor for who they are today and explore that. My case study financial executive chose the cinematic *Die Hard* character John McClane, played by Bruce Willis, as a present-day metaphor for his alter ego. While rejecting the cartoonish and violent attributes of this character, the metaphor confirmed a preference for fast thinking followed by action in stressful situations which would be immediately significantly beneficial for others.

Working in the past and present with the client builds their self-awareness, which of course is key to understanding their identity.

The Gestalt Empty Chair Technique

Before we look at how we go to the future to understand how our client will become more of their best self, let me share a technique here which is useful in helping a client who has difficulty with any of the preceding exercises. For example, the client may not be able to readily access their emotions and skills used during the resonant event in question. Or they may not have the language to describe their feelings and skills there. The MetaView, or looking deeper at what is going on in a situation from a different perspective (rather than why something is or is not happening) is a very effective technique for coaching your client over these difficulties.

A more in-depth explanation of using metaphors to get a different perspective and their role in coaching can be found in Chapter 1: 'Turn Your Challenge Inside OUT: The Physical Metaphor Technique' by Veronica Munro and Richard Haggerty.

To do this, we use the Gestalt Empty Chair technique, and move them to another chair where we can get them to imagine they are observing their current self from a different perspective. We ask them questions about their selves in the empty chair from this new position:

- *What is going on for you in this place?*
- *What skills were you using in that place?*
- *Were you happy, sad, angry, satisfied, peaceful, stressed in that place?*
- *What words would you use to describe how you felt, not what you thought?*
- *What can you see from here, that you couldn't see from there?*

- *What keeps you stuck in that place?*
- *Who are you in that place?*
- *How could you move forward?*

Or we can get them to use their imagination, and imagine that they have helicoptered up above themselves, and are now looking down. We can ask the same questions from this different perspective.

3. COACHING THE FUTURE

We can now look at the last of the trio, the future, and coaching there to help our client.

Visualisation: imagining the future

To take our client into the future and help them to discover their best self there, to know more about who they are becoming, we use visualisation. Here we ask our client to imagine an ideal future, where they are doing what they love to do.

To help them visualise this future place more effectively we might again get them to physically move to a new chair or part of the room as so often a physical shift causes a mental shift. Explain that a physical shift can often cause a mental shift that can reveal new insights and ideas. Then ask them if they would they like to explore that option with you now. Either invite them to select the place in the room that best represents the future for them or invite them to move to another chair.

In this place we can ask them questions similar to those we asked when exploring the past:

- *Where are you?*
- *Who are you with?*
- *What are you doing?*

- *How do you feel there in the future?*
- *Who have you become there?*
- *How are you different there in the future?* Again, we can invite them into an encounter with Higher Power / Hero to bring that perspective into the picture.
- *What have they become aware of there in the future that they were not aware of in the present?*

What are their answers to identity clarifying questions such as:

- *How does the Higher Power / Hero see you there?*

It is key in this future exercise that your client is enjoying the visualisation, and that you get them to be very specific about the future.

Metaphor is very helpful when supporting the client in coaching the future:

- *What have you become aware of there in the future that you were not aware of in the present?*
- *What metaphor comes to mind now in your future?*

Finally, we can ask our client: *What is the one action you want to take in the present moment to start the journey towards making this a future reality?* In our case study the financial executive chose to make time to explore possible careers with international charities and rescue organisations as a Crisis Project Manager / Director as a first step and ultimately left Financial Services for a new career in crisis management. His colleagues, family and friends have commented (as has he) on how this move has brought out his best qualities and that all feel he is now living his real identity and purpose.

We can also work with values and desires at any of the stages (past, present, or future) in order to reveal more of their identity.

For more tools on working with values in coaching, see Chapter 9: 'Values: Developing a Powerful Guidance System' by David Ross.

Coaching insights and summary

This chapter has revealed the value and power of clients knowing their identity more deeply as unique people. People who have an identity far greater than just what they do. As the saying goes – 'we are human beings, not human doings.'

It shared coaching tools that can be used to explore resonant moments in the client's past, present and future to reveal to them a deep self-awareness of their attributes, desires, personality, character and values that make up who they are today and who they are becoming as they grow. It increases their current performance and future potential. Clear identity gives clients freedom to select current and future roles which allow them to make their greatest contribution to their teams, organisations and the wider world by being authentic and clear about who they are. The world greatly benefits from people who are grounded about their identity and what they are called to do, who can help address its most difficult problems and greatest opportunities. I therefore encourage you to try this approach with one of your own clients to see its power for yourself.

Footnotes

Permission was given to write this chapter using Tina Southgate's proprietary, innovative coaching model to coach identity. For more information on Tina's models on coaching identity visit www.coachingidentity.com

Further resources
Richard N. Bolles, *What color is your parachute?* (Ten Speed Press, 2019)
Ken Robinson, *The element: how finding your passion changes everything* (Penguin, 2009)
Further coaching identity eCourses, training programmes and resources are available via www.tinasouthgate.com

~

Connect with the Author
Thank you for taking the time to read this chapter. I hope you have found it worthwhile. I would appreciate any feedback you might have for me on this topic and approach. If you would like to be coached in this way or are looking for a coaching provider who can help clients at depth, please contact me, Aidan Tod, at aidan@12exec.co.uk or visit www.twelveexecutivecoaching.co.uk

V

THE SOUL

Covered in this section

Now we arrive at the core, the inner essence of a person, where coaching is totally fearless and arrives at the deepest levels of a client's being – the journey inside.

What does it mean to be working at the most profound levels inside a person, and what can that achieve? How deep and transformative can coaching really go? Being an elite level coach and leader means being able to work intuitively and flexibly at multiple levels of the unconscious mind and with a very wide variety of techniques: linguistics, behaviour shaping, personality filters, mindfulness, neuro processing, emotional foot printing, high levels of sensory acuity, and the ability to be creative in the moment whilst keeping completely focused on the internal experience of the client (as they are being coached) are all examples of skills coaches draw upon at this level.

Chapter 11: The Soul: Coaching to the Core
Veronica Munro

In this chapter we journey even deeper into another human being's core, into their soul – the essence of a living being. Veronica guides us through a powerful process to go deeply and fully with clients to places they may never otherwise get to, and demonstrates the transformational nature of coaching, particularly when a strong relationship of trust is forged.

We learn the anatomy of the challenges clients may experience through a compelling case study, and see how all the elements of their personality and psyche have changed.

Veronica also elegantly demonstrates how to integrate and use all the diverse coaching models in the book, and where coaches, mentors and leaders may choose to use these in the process of coaching to the core.

THE SOUL

Coaching to the Core

Veronica Munro

For any lasting change to take place within another human being there needs to be the motivation to change something. That something, a way of being, a behaviour, a belief, or whatever, has become so powerful within a person that there are now significant negative consequences impacting different areas of their life. In fact its very existence has led this client to you, possibly in a state of emergency.

In this chapter we are going to journey deeper into another human being's psyche into their soul – the incorporeal essence of a living being.

We will explore 5 steps to coaching the soul, followed by a powerful case study to show just how impactful this type of coaching can be.

The 5 steps for coaching the soul are both stages, and guiding principles, to help you navigate as you coach to the core:

1. The Invitation
2. Purpose and approach
3. Processing
4. Aftercare
5. Diagnosis and reinventing.

1. THE INVITATION

Knowing we are being invited to work at the soul level, at the essence of who someone is

When someone says 'I'm going to tell you something that I have never told anyone else before,' this is a clear indicator (and flag) that the client has never had this conversation with someone before in their life; it is therefore a bold move on their part, and requires increased sensitivity, sensory acuity and compassion on the part of the coach. Topics prefaced with these kinds of comments have typically touched people at the deepest and most profound levels. On hearing what they have to say we may or may not be surprised at the significance, or otherwise, of what they share; however, we must always respect what their story means to them.

The client starts to lead the coaching by sharing the deepest aspects of their life, their feelings, their hang-ups, and their most significant and entrenched personal challenges etc. At the beginning the coach may seek to tread carefully and wait for the client to open up a few more doors inside themselves and show us what is *behind* them. Much of this information is also new to the client, as it has never been explored before. They have never told these things to anyone else, and so they have probably never heard themselves say it out loud. Just vocalising their story will begin to stimulate their emotions and thoughts as they order these and share them with you. They may also feel vulnerable, so it is essential for the coach to go slowly, listen and be patient in order to build trust and avoid triggering any defence mechanisms. Once trust and rapport is established we can then assist our clients, not only to find further doors inside themselves, but also to open them.

The client may let us know about their mental and physical pains, their desperation, sadness and the mess they are in, for example, with their personal relationships.

The client is sometimes unable to identify any area of their life where they feel happy. This again is an indicator, or clue, that we are witnessing the depths of another human being.

2. PURPOSE AND APPROACH

The purpose of coaching the soul and how to approach it

The purpose is to help connect, or re-connect, the person to their soul with the aim of creating inner alignment within the whole self to create happiness and well-being.

It is important to invite your client to name this part. (Do not label it yourself; it belongs to them, not you.) Whatever word or name they choose, for example spirit, soul or 'Harry,' use that word throughout your coaching with them. In the case study below, you will see that my client chooses the word 'soul.'

There are a number of ways to approach coaching the soul. One approach is for the coach to invite the client to imagine sitting inside themselves next to their soul and ask it some questions. This deepens their understanding of themselves and the work they wish to do. For instance:

- *How is your soul feeling?*
- *What does it want to tell you? Listen to it.*
- *What does it want or need from you? Listen.*
- *What else does it wish to share with you at this time?*
- *What does it look like?*

- *What would you like to say to your soul at this moment?*
- *Is there anything else that needs to be said or shared?*

By supporting them to communicate with their soul, they start to understand what it is they want and need and what changes they seek to make. You may wish to share with your client that the 'soul' communicates with us in many different ways – through images, metaphors, pictures, colours, and through physical feelings within the body (e.g. a pain in the neck, a tightness in the stomach, a lump in the throat). This means that we, as coaches, need to be comfortable and are able to work with the metaphors that clients present to us. If we are not, this is something we can bring to supervision or take training in, so as to deepen our practice. Of course as professional coaches we will not coach outside our capabilities.

3. PROCESSING

What happens when the soul is processing thoughts, feelings, images and memories

The soul communicates through our whole being via thoughts, feelings, images, sounds and the physical body. It is helpful for clients to acknowledge and pay attention to these 'messages,' listening to them, seeking to understand them and identifying their deepest needs and wants.

For example, one of my clients was having huge battles within himself, with his family and with his work colleagues. It was his boss who suggested that he have some executive coaching as he was leading a sizeable part of the company in Europe and needed to be at his best as a leader, rather than ranting at others on a regular basis. I invited the client to picture a metaphor of what it felt like being him in his current situation. He immediately transported himself back to the trenches in wartime Wales in the early Middle Ages. He was fighting for his life with an axe in his hand fending off his attackers. It was a Welsh rebellion and he very clearly described the mud and blood covering the tunic he was wearing. Our work together started from this point with this key 'message' from his soul.

Another example of how the 'soul' communicates with us was a young woman, the youngest financial director this particular organisation had ever had. She was experiencing serious levels of stress which were resulting in some health issues that were also impacting her relationships with her family, as well as her colleagues. Her psychologist had diagnosed that she was seriously depressed, though she was not on any medication at this time. Her life was completely filled with work and she could not identify any areas of her life that were fun or pleasurable.

I invited her to picture her challenge as a metaphor. She closed her eyes and imagined herself walking. She had a huge sense of loneliness and felt more and more buried in her life. There were dark clouds above her, though there was no rain. The earth was bone dry and nothing grew where she was. Soon she had reached the centre of the earth where she felt the weight of the world on her shoulders. This was the starting point for our work together.

The final session with this client started again at the centre of the earth, but now her images were transformed. Now, she was a little girl (aged around five) in a colourful dress standing in the sunshine holding onto a colourful bunch of helium balloons. The sky was clear and blue. She then started marching out of the centre of the earth followed by a big brass band playing uplifting and happy music. She felt happy, alive and free to be herself.

This uplifting image has stayed with her throughout her career and life and continues to be a key part of who she is.

It is essential for us as coaches to be open enough to these significant metaphors and happenings within our clients, and to be able to do the work with them, wherever they appear and however they represent our clients' internal worlds.

Coaches also need to become familiar with how to deal with a client who is crying. It is a natural cathartic process for the body to release, and let go of, pent up energy, emotions and stress. The body literally 'cries' out about what it fears, what it has lost and what it wants. It is a natural healing process that releases and removes toxins from the body which, in turn, reduces stress. It is also important for the client to feel that it is OK to cry in front of you. What you as a coach can do is pass a tissue box and say and do nothing. The work is being done *inside* the client and does not require you to say, or do, anything as this might interfere with what they are processing. Once they stop, let them speak first.

4. AFTERCARE

Looking after a client's well-being

It is important after any deep level work to ensure that the client puts their well-being first and has the time to think and process what has happened directly after the session. Taking care for one client, for example, was inviting him to have a long quiet walk by himself in the park before going to have something to eat and then returning home to his family. He also decided to leave his phone off for the rest of the afternoon and early evening. As the coach your role here might be to coach and facilitate the client to give themselves permission to do this, as their planned schedule may be calling them loudly back to the office. You will be able to show them that taking care of themselves right now is the best thing for them, their team and organisation.

These interventions take time for the client to process, and continue to be processed outside their conscious awareness, at the unconscious level, for days and sometimes weeks afterwards. Running off straight away to join a meeting, have a call or check in on emails etc can interfere with this processing and therefore should be avoided immediately after these interventions. Arranging your sessions with clients right before lunch or towards the end of the day, when the client is most likely able to take a break, can be helpful.

5. DIAGNOSIS AND REINVENTING

Building range and flexibility in your coaching skills and approaches

Throughout this book you will have come across a varied range of coaching interventions. I am sure you will have your own favourites too. Any of these may be appropriate and helpful for coaching at this level, and you get to choose the right one at the right time to suit the client's situation and challenge. One size does not fit all. By learning as many different styles and approaches to coaching as you can, you have the freedom to select the most appropriate interventions or techniques for your client's individual needs and that fit your own personality and coaching style.

Health warning! A newly qualified dentist had just acquired a specialist drill. Guess what all his patients were diagnosed with for the following few weeks? Tooth decay, that required extensive drilling and filling. Make sure you aren't mesmerised by the latest techniques you learn. Flexibility, creativity and generative coaching is the way forward for the highest impact and deepest sustainable change in our clients.

The case study below is a summary of the work I completed with a client named George.

Following this I have included a table which details some of the early diagnostics from his coaching sessions, the 'reinvented' George and the new resources he acquired following the coaching, and links to the relevant chapters and approaches in this book that you may choose to use at each stage of the coaching process when coaching the soul.

CASE STUDY: GEORGE

'I'm going to tell you something that I have never told anyone else' said George.

George was a very interesting and different client for me in the early stages of my career as an executive coach. He was part of the leadership team of a highly successful global pharmaceutical company and was invited, along with everyone else, to have some executive coaching. We met for the first time at their city offices on a cold, dark, damp winter's day. He sat across the desk from me in his round spectacles, curly dark hair, and a pinstripe suit with a neatly buttoned up waistcoat beneath his jacket. Before I opened my mouth to say hello he insisted he didn't want or need a coach. 'I have a coach you know' he said. 'I have had one for FIVE years and see him twice a week.' 'Ah' I said. 'Yes! And I know all about myself. I have been studying myself for years now,' he continued. 'Ah' I said. 'Yes! My friend also has a coach. He has had one for 10 years.' 'Really' I said. 'Have you changed at all in those five years with all those coaching sessions?' 'Changed! Of course I HAVEN'T CHANGED!' 'Ah' I said. 'Well coaching IS about change and moving forward.' George sat back and looked shocked. He huffed and puffed, and looked seriously annoyed with himself. He later told me he had just realised how much time he may have wasted over the last five years lying on a sofa at his coach's (in fact therapist's) office. 'So! What have you got to offer then?' he asked grumpily and that is where we started.

The trigger for his 'coaching' five years ago was the suicide of his brother for which he had assumed responsibility. He became extremely depressed, went to a doctor who provided him with some anti-depressants and then he found himself a 'shrink.' Someone to 'shrink' his pain away for him. Though this obviously hadn't worked for him.

George was aching inside. He told me that he wanted to be happy and didn't know how to be. His personal relationships with his wife, his young family and people around him were on a knife's edge. He just wasn't able to relate to anyone, including himself. With the help of medication and his 'coach' he had managed to repress his feelings about his brother's suicide. Or at least that is what he had been trying to do.

I explained the coaching model I would use with him and mentioned that we could work at the conscious / cognitive level initially so that he could learn some new skills and techniques. However, it would not be possible to work effectively at the deeper levels due to his medication, which was acting as a numbing agent and barrier to change at the deeper levels. (I had professional advice about this from my supervisor and a qualified therapist, so I was comfortable working with him in this way.)

George understood and decided to work with me anyway.

George and I quickly built a trusting relationship. He shared his deepest darkest secrets with me and then we reached the end of this part of his coaching. Pacing him was critical at this juncture. This was a man who by his own admission had lost his way and was deeply unhappy in many aspects of his life: his family, his work, his health, his relationships and his sense of purpose for his life. He was miserable. He asked if I would work with him when he was off the medication as he wanted to face the pain, the tears, and the hurt, and change his life around. I agreed to work with him and asked him to consult with his doctor and therapist and gain their advice on next steps and the best way for him to come off the anti-depressants. I suggested he take his time and get in touch with me when he was ready.

Four months later, George called. He booked a private meeting room away from the office in the morning and arranged to have the rest of the day off work. This was a wise choice as working with him on his deepest emotions about his brother's suicide was going to be a significant and potentially highly emotional piece of work, so having time to himself afterwards would allow him to unconsciously process more fully the work we were going to do. George desperately needed and wanted a conversation with his deceased younger brother to help him live with his death. I therefore chose to use the Gestalt 'Empty Chair

Technique,'[1] although in his case he stood up throughout. When we prepared together, George imagined his deceased brother coming into the room. I then invited George to have the conversation he wanted with his brother, either out loud or inside his own head. He stood and had the conversation silently inside his own head and he cried and cried and cried.

I sat apart from George and his brother, guided him through the process and otherwise remained silent. His whole body was crying. After some time talking with his brother, he stopped, said farewell to him and then sunk back into the large chair in the room. He was exhausted.

Now was the time for some 'aftercare' following the session. In this case, I waited for George to 'come back into the room' and settle. It was my duty to ensure that George stepped back into 'the real world' of 'here and now' feeling stronger and more grounded. We did some simple re-resourcing of his body and soul, as well as some 'state management.' He practised the disposition of 'Stability' (Newfield Network)[2] as he walked around the large room feeling and thinking like a king.

---

1   Empty Chair Technique from Gestalt therapy that was developed by Fritz Perls, Laura Perls and Paul Goodman in the 1940s and 1950s, and was first described in 1951 in *Gestalt Therapy* (The Gestalt Journal Press, 1951).
2   Newfield Network, '4 body dispositions (Somatics),' https://newfieldnetwork.com/wp-content/uploads/2016/09/Syllabus_Newfield-CCT_USA_201608.pdf

It was important for him to be on his own for a while, not doing anything in particular, just allowing himself to enjoy some fresh air, a walk, a cup of coffee or whatever, on his own. This period on his own was time for his unconscious mind and his whole body to process the changes he had been making, without any interruptions or interference. This allowed his mind time to let go, to relax and avoid talking to anyone about anything, and in particular about the intervention.

Following this powerful intervention George decided he wanted to do further coaching that would enable him to live his life fully and 'reinvent' himself to be the person he wanted to be. George's story concludes below.

CASE STUDY SUMMARY

Below is a table that outlines aspects of George's identity and challenges that we worked with. In the three separate columns you will find:

1. The original diagnostics; the problem areas that were not working for George

2. The 'reinvented' George along with the new resources he acquired and shifts he made during the coaching following the significant intervention relating to his brother, and

3. The combination and range of interventions used with George that enabled him to make the shifts to new ways of being, new beliefs, revised values, new emotions, behaviours and skills to the new George that he wanted to be, along with the resources to do so.

Table 11.1: George's journey

George: original diagnostics	Reinventing himself with new resources	References to interventions in this book
Identity: Way of Being		
• I am going to survive on my own (runs across all contexts)	• I am living my life to the full	• Read 'Coaching for Identity Grows Purpose and Performance' by Aidan Tod • Read 'Ways Of Being: The Way to Be Who You Want to Be' by David Ross
Beliefs	**New beliefs**	
• I am responsible for my brother's death. It's my fault • This pain and hurt are here to stay. Feeling hurts	• I love life • I choose how I feel each and every day • I always do the best I can (and so do others)	• Read 'Take the Plunge and Dive Deeper using Transactional Analysis' by Shirley Attenborough

• I am lonely and on my own • I didn't / don't love my brother and family enough • It's easier for me to be on my own and not be hurt	• I respect other people's models of the world • I love my family • I have the ability to build relationships with people that are loving and productive • I build on my strengths and leverage the strengths of others	• Read 'Breaking Free: Unlocking Doors with Deep Reframing' by Richard Haggerty
Emotions		
• Anger • Sadness • Fear of being hurt	• Shifting from emotions that were not serving him to emotions that do • (See States below)	• Read 'Getting to the Heart of the Matter: Emotions-Centred Coaching' by Dan Newby

Values		
• Independence • Loyalty • (No Value on relationships – all interactions with people are transactions to keep people at arms' length) • Money • Career Progression • Results	• Life • Fun • Results • Make a difference • Relationships • Applied to self and to others (two-way lens) and generalised across all contexts	• Read 'Values: Developing a Powerful Guidance System' by David Ross

Skills		
• Observation of people to anticipate whether they will hurt me or my family • Project management – good at managing stuff on my own	• Learn how to achieve win / win outcomes as I continually build effective relationships	• Read 'The Transformational Impact of Active Listening' by Colin D. Smith

• Persuasion skills – determined to get what wanted – sell outcome rather than bring them on board – forced people to follow my way of thinking • Communication + presenting	• Respect other people's model of the world • Building rapport • Active Listening • Pacing others • Linguistics / language • Organise my activities to deliver on my priorities • Communication and Influence	• Read 'Turn Your Challenge Inside OUT: The Physical Metaphor Technique' by Veronica Munro and Richard Haggerty
Behaviours		
• Dissociation (separating) from my feelings • Listening for how I could persuade	• Associate to my feelings and the feelings of others (depending on circumstances)	• Read 'Getting to the Heart of the Matter: Emotions-Centred Coaching' by Dan Newby

• Language of Influence • Smile on my face	• Watching and listening deeply • Balanced use of energy • Pay attention to my own state to ensure productive state for what is happening around me	• Read 'The Transformational Impact of Active Listening' by Colin D. Smith
States		
• Anxiety (always on edge) • Sadness • Hurt	• Calm • Confident and strong • Energised • Clarity of thinking • Caring for myself and others	• Read 'Coaching the Unconscious Mind through Metaphor' by Richard Haggerty

Being at your best when coaching to the core

When something profound and important surfaces for your client, you, as their coach, need to adopt a particular mindset and approach that is uniquely your own and truly authentic. Pacing your client throughout the session is critical, as it is in all coaching sessions. Here are some general principles:

- Choose your own state – how do you want to be?
- Listen with your heart
- Allow the person to be
- Allow yourself to be as the client leads you
- Say and ask little, or nothing at all
- Leave space for the client to consider what else they wish to tell you
- Slow down your pace and energy (go into a lower gear) to help the client slow down too and explore more deeply inside themselves.

Coaching 21.3 grams

In 1901 Duncan MacDougall (an American physician) conducted a number of experiments in which he weighed a person just before, and then immediately after, they died. He found that a person weighed approximately 21.3 grams *less* after they died. From this he concluded that the soul, which had left the body at death, weighed approximately 21.3 grams. That is just .75 of an ounce. Although the research was done with a very small sample size and was criticised by peers, it tapped into the Zeitgeist, and has subsequently become a powerful metaphor of how small and precious the deepest part of ourselves, and our lives, are.

You may wish to consider in your mind that you are holding someone's soul in your hands, all 21.3 grams of it. The life force of another being. They have entrusted you to do this. Hold it delicately, and with respect.

Coaching conclusion: George

Only six months after George had completed his executive coaching and 'reinvention,' he was promoted to the board of the organisation as a leading light in his field. His relationships with his wife and his children were back on track and they were all thrilled and enjoying family times together once again. George, for the first time in almost six years, was happy within himself and with his life.

George's personal relationships are not fully detailed in this case study. What is true though is that his relationships with others mirrored his relationship with himself. As do ours. When the outside is not working for us, we need to look at the inside to begin our journey, coaching to the core.

~

Connect with the Author

Thank you for reading this chapter. If you would like to understand more about this coaching stance and techniques for 'coaching the soul,' to connect, or to explore deepening your coaching skills so that you are working at the 'top of your game,' please contact me at results@veronicamunro.com and visit www. veronicamunro.com

Every interaction between people leaves an emotional footprint and an impact, whether we like it or not!
May yours be as you intended

May your soul shine
your words fly
your smile warm
as you change the world
one person at a time

ABOUT THE CONTRIBUTORS

Shirley Attenborough

Shirley has an MSc in occupational psychology, and is a leadership coach with over twenty years' international experience. She has designed and facilitated accredited coaching programmes and leadership workshops. Her clients include leading business schools, some of the top consultancy firms, as well as CEOs of multinational companies. Her coaching approach is eclectic, and she uses a variety of techniques from different disciplines. She enjoys supporting her clients to experiment with different strategies and behaviours in order to achieve their full potential. For more information contact shirleyattenborough@gmail.com

Richard Haggerty

Richard is the developer of Deep Reframing and Unconscious Coaching Methodologies (UCM). An experienced coach, trainer and presenter, he is renowned for creating profound transformation for clients globally. With a focus on creating bespoke programmes that coach the unconscious mind, he has been integrating hypnosis and Neuro-Linguistic Programming (NLP) into coaching for two decades to enable clients to access new ways of thinking, acting and being that achieve inspired results. Richard is known for his warm, passionate and inspiring client-focused approach, and belief that Deep Transformation is always possible with the right strategies, motivation and commitment. For more information visit www.RichardHaggerty. co.uk

Veronica Munro

Veronica is an international executive and leadership coach, strategic facilitator, conference speaker and author who works across the globe with CEOs, senior executives and their teams in leading multi-national companies. As a senior leader herself working at the highest levels within organisations, her strengths include her strategic, commercial and practical approach to coaching that leaders find effective and refreshing. She thereby facilitates leadership growth, alignment and sustainable behavioural change that delivers improved levels of business performance and results. A CEO recently wrote the following on Veronica's impactful coaching: 'The best way that sums up such a working relationship is "life changing".' For more information visit www.veronicamunro.com or email results@veronicamunro.com

Dan Newby

Dan is an advocate for emotional literacy globally through his books, workshops, presentations and educational materials. He teaches coaches, educators and leaders to understand and leverage their emotional intelligence. He is trained as an educator, spent twenty years as a business entrepreneur and leader before moving into the world of coaching. Dan is a passionate teacher and loves supporting his students in developing their emotional competence and skills. He lives near Barcelona, Spain with his co-author and wife, Lucy Núñez. His books include *The Unopened Gift: A Primer in Emotional Literacy*; *21 Days to Emotional Literacy: A Companion Workbook to the Unopened Gift*; and *The Field Guide to Emotions: A Practical Orientation to 150 Essential Emotions*. He can be contacted at dan@schoolofemotions.world

David Ross

David Ross is the developer of Six Steps to Unlimited Performance, a coaching model designed to deliver transformational behavioural change and specific measurable results within a three- to six-month window. With over 30 years building his expertise, David has trained and certified hundreds of coaches in the Six Step model. He has worked extensively with CEOs and the leadership teams of multi-nationals enabling them to develop to their full potential. David is passionate about connecting people and strategy, enabling them to optimise sustainable results through strong leadership. Today, David is passionate about supporting charities to develop strategies enabling them to realise long-term impact in making the difference they choose to make to other people's lives. For more information, email david.ross@cloud9apps.co.uk

Colin D. Smith

Colin D. Smith, aka The Listener, is an executive coach and confidant, speaker, and passionate about transforming the way we listen. His calm, attentive and patient way of being, enables you to feel seen, heard and understood. It awakens your thinking and inspires you to empathically listen to yourself and others. His approach is not about fixing, offering advice (unless asked), or rescuing you. He creates a safe, compassionate place for you to slow down, settle, and be yourself. In this space, you are able to listen to your innermost thoughts and feelings, out of which your true story and answers will emerge. www.dexteritysolutions.co.uk

Aidan Tod

Aidan is a senior executive coach and has worked impactfully with executives for over 30 years as a people specialist and coach across different sectors and countries. Energised by finding his own vocation and purpose in coaching, and encouraging executives to be their very best self, he loves to assist others wishing to find their own passion and purpose. His website www.twelveexecutivecoaching.co.uk shares resources for leaders interested in growing themselves and their contribution to their organisations and the world. Aidan would like to thank Tina Southgate, master coach, www.tinasouthgate.com for the use of her coaching identity model in this book.

Printed in Great Britain
by Amazon